DISCLAIMER AND TERMS OF USE AGREEMENT

The author and publisher of this book have used their best efforts in preparing this book. The author and publisher make no representation or warranties with respect to the accuracy, applicability, fitness, or completeness of the contents of this book. The information contained in this book is strictly for educational purposes.

Therefore, if you wish to apply ideas contained in this book, you are taking full responsibility for your actions.

The author and publisher disclaim any warranties (express or implied), merchantability, or fitness for any particular purpose. The author and publisher shall in no event be held liable to any party for any direct, indirect, punitive, special, incidental or other consequential damages arising directly or indirectly from any use of this material, which is provided "as is", and without warranties.

As always, the advice of a competent legal, tax, accounting, medical or other appropriate professional should be sought.

The author and publisher do not warrant the performance, effectiveness or applicability of any sites listed or linked to in this book or accompanying materials.

All links are for information purposes only and are not warranted for content, accuracy or any other implied or explicit purpose.

This book is © copyrighted by Jennifer Longmore and Soul Journeys®. No part of this may be copied, or changed in any format, sold, or used in any way other than what is outlined within this book under any circumstances.

ISBN 978-1-5085-4331-2

88 UNIVERSAL LAWS

by Jennifer Longmore

North America's Soul Purpose Expert
CEO of SoulJourneys.ca

88 UNIVERSAL LAWS

by Jennifer Longmore

North America's Soul Purpose Expert
CEO of SoulJourneys.ca

Table of Contents

INTRODUCTION 7

1. The Law of Abundance 8
2. The Law of Action 9
3. The Law of Akasha 9
4. The Law of Analogy 10
5. The Law of Ascension 10
6. The Law of Attraction 11
7. The Law of Balance 12
8. The Law of Challenge 12
9. The Law of Cohesion 12
10. The Law of Colour 13
11. The Law of Common Ground 13
12. The Law of Consciousness 13
13. The Law of Continuity of Consciousness 14
14. The Law of Cycles 14
15. The Law of Divine Invocation 15
16. The Law of Discipline 15
17. The Law of Divine Flow 16
18. The Law of Divine Love and Oneness 17
19. The Law of Economy 17
20. The Law of Economy of Force 17
21. The Law of Equalities *(or Analogy)* *18*
22. The Law of Expansion 19
23. The Law of Expectation 19
24. The Law of Faith 19
25. The Law of Flexibility 20
26. The Law of Forgiveness 21
27. The Law of Free Will 22

88 UNIVERSAL LAWS

28. The Law of Gender 22
29. The Law of Good Will 23
30. The Law of Grace 24
31. The Law of Group Endeavour 24
32. The Law of Group Life 25
33. The Law of Healing 26
34. The Law of Higher Will 26
35. The Law of Honesty 27
36. The Law of Identity 27
37. The Law of Intention 28
38. The Law of Intuition 28
39. The Law of Justice 28
40. The Law of Karma 29
41. The Law of Knowledge 30
42. The Law of Love 30
43. The Law of Magnetic Control 31
44. The Law of Magnetic Impulse 31
45. The Law of Magnetism 31
46. The Law of Manifestation 32
47. The Law of Mantras 32
48. The Law of Meditation 32
49. The Law of Process 33
50. The Law of Mentalism 33
51. The Law of Miracles 33
52. The Law of No Judgments 34
53. The Law of Non-Attachment 34
54. The Law of Non-Intervention 35
55. The Law of One 35
56. The Law of Order of Creation 36
57. The Law of Patience 36
58. The Law of Patterns 36
59. The Law of Perfection 37

60. The Law of Periodicity 38
61. The Law of Polarity 38
62. The Law of the Present Moment 39
63. The Law of Progress 39
64. The Law of Prophecy 39
65. The Law of Radiation 40
66. The Law of Rebirth 40
67. The Law of Rebound 41
68. The Law of Responsibility 41
69. The Law of Rhythm 41
70. The Law of Right Human Relations 42
71. The Law of Schools *(The Law of Love & Light)* 43
72. The Law of Service 43
73. The Law of Solar Evolution 44
74. The Law of Sound 44
75. The Law of Spiritual Approach 44
76. The Law of Spiritual Awakening 45
77. The Law of Summons 45
78. The Law of Surrender 46
79. The Law of Synthesis 46
80. The Law of Teaching 46
81. The Law of Telepathy 47
82. The Law of Three Requests 47
83. The Law of Time 48
84. The Law of Unconditional Love 48
85. The Law of Unity 49
86. The Law of Vibration 49
87. The Law of Will of God 49
88. The Law of Will Power 50

PRACTICAL ASSIGNMENTS 51
ABOUT THE AUTHOR 59

INTRODUCTION

All creation is governed by laws - universal principles, if you will. The principles that operate in the outer universe, discoverable by scientists, are called natural laws. Some we can see, like the orbit of the stars and the changing of the seasons, while others, like gravity are invisible but exist beyond a doubt. We are energy, and what we say, think and do creates energy around us.

And there are subtler laws that rule the hidden spiritual planes and the inner realms of consciousness. Contained within these laws (or conditions) is the true nature of matter.

Knowledge of the laws that govern everything in the universe from the mighty cosmos to the tiny atom affects how you think, how you relate to the universe and others in it, and how the universe and others in it relate to you.

Love is the foundation of universal law: the mind the builder of your universe. The mind that is fully aware and attuned to the application of universal law in all matters is the mind that knows that in love all life is given, in love all things move.

Every action has an equal and opposite reaction. Every yin has its yang. Thus, in giving one attains. In giving one acquires. In giving, love becomes the fulfillment of desire, guided and directed in the ways that bring the more perfect knowledge of self as related to the universal, all powerful, all guiding, all divine influence in life. Love IS life. To give IS to receive.

When we go back, merge with the God Source, in some infinitesimal but profound way, we expand the Mind of God.

Our God is manifest in our and higher selves and always points to the best and most perfect way. It is ours to listen and accept or reject what we hear. God does not blame, but patiently tries again to show the perfect way, the loving way. All of creation pushes forth. – As we listen we are ever becoming. Identity ever remains!

1. The Law of Abundance

Why do some people seem to 'come up smelling like roses' regardless what happens to them? Why do others who make more effort make less progress in achieving their goals?

Also known as the Law of Opulence and the Law of Success, the Law of Abundance speaks to all we have in our lives on the inner and outer, social, emotional, and spiritual levels.

The law of abundance reveals that our wishes do come true, whether we wish poorly or we wish well. It does not apply only to money and material well-being, for indeed, there are many kinds of wealth and abundance manifests itself in many ways. The man who looks proudly on his children is wealthy, as is the woman who doesn't 'have it all' but is truly happy with who she is and 'all she has'.

We can have a wealth of common sense, understanding, and kindness. Or we can have the opposite. The choice is ours. We can manifest the wealth we want in our lives, but we must be mindful that we are much more than the sum-total of our possessions. When creating the abundance of financial gain we must remember to be IN this world, but not OF this world.

2. The Law of Action

No matter how strongly we feel what we feel or how much faith we have in what we know, feelings and knowledge are fruitless unless we act upon them. We may understand concepts such as commitment, courage, and love, but we do not know them until we act. Knowledge is action; doing becomes understanding. Our gifts and talents are only latent possibilities until we bring them to life.

Every aspirant is the focal point of energy in the midst of a whirlwind of energy, the chaos of the third dimension. Every aspirant must make his or her presence felt through action.

The universe responds to action. When we take deliberate action on behalf of something that we wish to create/change/shift, the universe observes this as readiness, and then brings you what you have now demonstrated you can handle. Remember: the universe *never* gives you what you can't handle!

3. The Law of Akasha

Akasha, the fifth and quintessential element, is the unifying force of the universe manifested in the intelligence of substance. Everything in the universe operates within the realm of unerring law because everything emanates from the same source energy. We are all 'one spirit' and all part and parcel of the cosmos, subject to the law of Akasha. The individual who lives in harmony with the universal force 'goes with the flow,' and all things prosper for she is riding the wave of creation.

In humans, Akasha refers to our ethereal spirit-being that cannot be seen but truly defines us as individuals. It is our interaction with the universal spirit, whether we tend it or neglect it, not 'life' or 'luck' that ultimately determines our fate.

4. The Law of Analogy

How is the universe like a hurricane? The energy infusing the universe manifests itself at every level in a multitude of different but analogous ways, and these analogies can be used to further understanding at all levels. The sweeping arc of the universe pictured from afar is 'the same' as the sweeping arc of a hurricane bearing down on land. An emotional storm in life is a whirlwind of violent emotion often called a 'perfect storm' or a 'hurricane'.

No analogy is ever exact as energy adapts itself to the moment, yet analogies enable us to explain the unexplainable by means of comparisons and this enables us to convey understanding in a broad sense.

5. The Law of Ascension

Think of yourself as a single string on a guitar. The other strings are the energy beings you attract, making up your life - the whole guitar. When strummed, whether poorly or well, each string resonates energy in the form of sound just as energy resonates from the soul of an incarnational being.

Those who are 'in tune' with universal energy and have lost the illusion that they are separated from the god-self, and they vibrate in harmony to the point of ascension. No longer does the incarnational personality wait to leave the earth-plane to achieve a finer or more harmonious existence, for 'heaven is here on earth'. The Law of Ascension means that we are meant to bring our loving energies to our everyday existence and to serve as models for others to emulate. We will recognize this ascendant energy in others by noting the degree to which other ascendant and non-ascendant beings are attracted to them.

6. The Law of Attraction

The Law of Attraction unites love and soul providing the universal harmony that is the foundation for all manifestation.

One of the Three Major Laws, the Law of Attraction is broken down into eleven subsidiary laws that compel the force of attraction holding our universe as well as our lives together. It is the Law of Attraction that holds our solar system to the Sirian and keeps our planets revolving around our central unit, the sun.

The Law of Attraction is the energy that spins the earth and holds molecular, atomic, and subatomic matter ever circulating around their centres. It is the primary law of man achieved through the synthesis of Love and Soul elements.

7. The Law of Balance

Also known as the Law of Fair Exchange, the Law of Balance or Equipoise is the law that supersedes all man's laws and creates stability for all third dimension manifestation. We get what we give; this is the principle of fair exchange.

Divine wisdom tells us that each thought must be balanced by the thinker. We must allow all viewpoints without letting the views of others dominate us, for each of us must make his own journey. Do not give away power easily, but give love unconditionally. Low self-esteem is just as non-productive as high self-esteem. They both deny equality. There is no salvation in extremes as we see in the manifestation of imbalance in addictive and compulsive personalities. Any message communicated with love validates equality and achieves balance.

8. The Law of Challenge

Just as there is a difference between being aggressive and being assertive, there is a difference between insulting and challenging a disembodied being.

When we encounter a disembodied being we have the right to ask his or her intent, identity, and whatever else we truly feel is pertinent. Those whose role it is to provide information to channelers do not mind being challenged, and if asked three times, in the same exact words each time, they will give accurate information.

9. The Law of Cohesion

Divine coherence is demonstrated in the molecular plane and manifested throughout the universe as the Law of Cohesion, one of the seven laws of the solar system. The Law of Cohesion is the source of universal unity and the home of the Monad.

10. The Law of Colour

Humans (hue-light; man-being) are composed of light, which in its purest sense, consists of colour, tone, symbol and vibration. All colours are centres of attraction whether they are complimentary or conflicting, and all colour impacts the physical, emotional, mental and human body profoundly. When rays of one or more colours are directed to a specific area of the body, change occurs.

11. The Law of Common Ground

Problems cannot be resolved by force or by compromise as one side invariably loses and will, as the saying goes, "come back to fight another day". The Law of Common Ground dictates that problems can be truly resolved when two or more ascendant beings gather together in a site that has been cleansed to blend their differences to reach a common goal.

Cleanse the area to be utilized of any residual energy from those who may have resided in or passed through it by caging it with a gold net and sending loving energy to the area for a period of time. This period will vary depending on who, historically speaking, has inhabited the space, the energy left behind, and the nature of the conflict you honestly wish to resolve. If the issue you wish to address is surrounded by contentious energy or residual negative energy inhabits the space, some time may be required.

12. The Law of Consciousness

As consciousness expands, so does our perspective; the space for events to transpire (possibility) increases and therefore the dimensions in which man recognizes good and evil, opportunity and possibility, past-present and future all expand to reveal the limits of prior perception and the real needs of this present world cycle.

13. The Law of Continuity of Consciousness

Cosmic consciousness creates an ever-expanding reality, and everything in creation is connected to everything else. The Universe is in a continuous and endless process of creation as the fusion of individual consciousness and the universal consciousness (the building of the antahkarana) results in the development of universal knowledge known as omniscience (all science/all knowledge). The medium for the 'implicit order' of this relationship is continuity. Achieving enlightenment requires that we be vigilant, observant of our context and surroundings in order to gain awareness of the larger context and to align ourselves within the cosmic continuity.

14. The Law of Cycles

As a part of nature we live within the pattern of larger cycles. We see them in the passing of seasons, in the continual passing of day to night, and in the waxing and waning of the moon. We cannot push the river; neither can we call back the tide. Universal timing is perfect, and all things that should happen, happen in 'good' time. It does not pay to despair or rejoice beyond measure for whatever rises falls, whatever fulls, empties. Nothing is forever; this is the principle of cycles.

15. The Law of Divine Invocation

"Under the Law of Grace" keeps us from unintentionally manifesting or invoking anything that would harm us, our karma and/or others. This law is not for the self-serving, for those want for self rather than for service will find the law overruled by self-interest.

For those who sincerely desire to do no harm and particularly for those working in the service of others, the Law of Divine Invocation allows the ascended realms to move from the confines of the Law of Non-Intervention to act on our behalf.

Invoke the Divine Decree three times by saying:

"By Divine Decree," in the name of _____ I ask for_____.

It is done and I thank you.

Or "Under the Law of Grace," in the name of _____ I ask for_____.

It is done and I thank you.

Repeat one (not both) of the request three times, and then let it go. Trust that it is in higher hands.

16. The Law of Discipline

Discipline is the surest means to the greatest freedom and independence.

Discipline enables us to focus and achieve the knowledge and skills that translate into more and better options in life. It is the muscle of the enlightened body, not because discipline is overbearing or rigid, but because it provides the strength of character and commitment that are the foundations of enlightened living. Discipline without commitment is a stab in the dark, not the bridge between here and where we want to be.

17. The Law of Divine Flow

"Ease up!" "Go with the flow!" "Get in synch!"—good advice for those stressed out and out of step with conscious living.

Living in the moment and centring ourselves in love and service to others (as opposed to service of self), we live within the Law of Divine Flow. When we stay in the moment by moment flowing of our higher selves, creating actions which reflect love and possibility, we notice how we say just the right things, do what is best for all, and refrain from doing that which we previously disliked in ourselves or others. We maintain a stronger connection to our God-self as we focus on the here-and-now rather than worrying about of trying to unduly manipulate the future. The more we do this, the more we are able to do this. To a degree, deliberately going against the flow means we have allowed our spiritual integrity to be compromised.

18. The Law of Divine Love and Oneness

When we, as ascendant beings, complete a round of reincarnation, we develop such soul growth that the vibrational speed of our being qualifies us to merge with God. We then become a soul extension of God, and among the many choices we have we may opt to live in the liquid light which flows in and from God, or reincarnate as an avatar in third dimensional existence with the purpose of aiding mankind.

19. The Law of Economy

The Law of Economy causes matter to always follow the line of least resistance, and this is the basis of the "separative" action of atomic matter atoms scatter from each other and in so doing create a vibratory rhythm attuned to the heterogeneity and quality inherent in rotary action. The Law of Economy governs matter and is the opposite pole of spirit. Initiates must master this law before they can achieve liberation and enlightenment.

20. The Law of Economy of Force

The initiate who aims to provide a point of contact between conditions of chaos and the initiate who works for constructive ends and order must ascribe to the Economy of Force in all they do. This requires due discrimination and a true sense of values. The result is the economizing of time and effort; energy is distributed wisely, excess is eliminated, and thus the aspirant can be relied upon by the Great Ones as a true and able helper.

One of the Three Major Laws, the Law of Economy of Force influences Activity. This is the law that adjusts the equilibrium between the material and spiritual evolution of the cosmos, ensuring that energy is expended to its best possible end with the minimum of force. Unevenness of rhythm is an illusion of time and does not exist in the cosmic centre which is perfectly balanced and aligned.

In knowing this, we find peace in all its connotations, peace that contains the next racial expansion of consciousness hidden within its meaning.

21. The Law of Equalities (or Analogy)

Experiential reality- life as we know it or think we know it, is but a reflection of the condition of the soul: our outer experience is basically equal to our innermost perception of ourselves and our place in the grand scheme of things. As within, so without. The thoughts and images we hold in our conscious and subconscious minds manifest their mirror likenesses in our external circumstances.

The Laws and Phenomena of the various planes of Being correspond to various aspects of life, and the Law of Equalities, also known as Principle of Correspondence or Essential Divinity enable the phenomena of Discernment, Intuition, Hunches, etc. and that which is called remote viewing or out of body experience. Earth is a school for practicing these laws of mind control while maintaining a connection to all being.

Correspondence establishes the interconnectedness between all things in the universe and keeps all things relative to each other. Known to the adepts and masters of ancient Egypt as the substance of the ethereal and the spirit substance or web that pervades and interpenetrates the universe, the substance of the ethereal acts as a medium for the transmission of light, heat, electricity and gravity. Non-material in nature, it is also known as the un-created substance, or universal substance.

First discovered on Earth while scientists were conducting research with the Hubble space telescope spirit-substance is manifesting in the ethers. It is the beginning of matter. This is the lifeforce in which all suns, worlds, and galaxies are suspended in space, time and change. Science refers to this substance as "dark matter" that cannot be seen, touched, smelled, or weighed. Dark matter does not absorb or reflect light and is therefore invisible. It is considered a non-material substance present in each of the three Planes of Correspondence, also known as the ascending scale of life and being and the Trinity of Being: The Great Spiritual Plane; The Great Mental Plane; The Great Physical Plane.

We are all intimately connected via this dark matter of essential being, whether we realize it or not. Dark matter is the source of love-wisdom and the major linking agent in the universe that leads us back toward the sense of oneness and enlightenment.

22. The Law of Expansion

It is a fact in nature that all existence dwells within a sphere. This is the law of a gradual evolutionary expansion. The consciousness dwelling in every life form is the cause of the spheroid-like form of all life in the solar system. The law of relativity, or the relation between all atoms, produces that which is called Light which in its aggregated phenomena, forms a composite sphere, known a solar system. The sphere requires two types of force - rotary and spiral-cyclic to produce its own internal activity.

The Law of Expansion is also known as the Law of Expansive Response, and its symbol is the flaming rosy sun with a sign symbolizing the union of fire and water in the centre. The ray energy is the expansive energy of the 3rd ray, the adapting factor.

23. The Law of Expectation

We can move toward what we can see, but we cannot exceed the bounds of our own imaginations. Energy follows thought thus allowing our deepest thoughts, for better or for worse, to manifest. Our fundamental assumptions, expectations and beliefs, however, colour and create our experience. Only by changing our fundamental expectations can we change our outcomes.

24. The Law of Faith

We know more than we know, we have hunches, intuitions, and visions of a whole that is larger than the sum of what we have read, heard or studied. Déjà vu is nothing more than the recollection of the larger collective unconscious: the universal ALL that we are all a part of.

Each of us, explains renowned psychologist, Carl Gustav Jung, holds a pool of collective, universal knowledge within our subconscious; this is universal knowledge. We have only to look within, listen, discern, and trust our inner, universal knowledge. We must learn to differentiate between our outward desires and biases to objectively access our deepest intuitions and to rely on intuitive knowledge as the ultimate arbitrator in all of our decisions. Faith in the collective body of universal knowledge is the key to the Law of Faith.

25. The Law of Flexibility

Acceptance of our selves and others for what they are without drama or bias means embracing and making constructive use of the moment—even if it wasn't our finest. It is the only moment that IS. Our actions and reactions define us.

Everything serves the highest good if we make the best possible use of it. This requires an alert and expansive state of awareness as well as the ability to lay ego to one side. Stumbling blocks become stepping stones and problems become opportunities. This is the basic foundation of personal growth and true spiritual development. We must have, as the Buddha advised and 12 step programs around the world remind us, "the serenity to accept the things we cannot change, the courage to change the things we can, and the wisdom to know the difference."

26. The Law of Forgiveness

When we see all as love we build the energy of allowingness we realize that in the full process of time, all things are forgiven. Thus we lose the need for retribution or revenge. By forgiving we release old anger and open the way for the Law of Grace to intercede and dispense away with negative karma we may have accumulated in the Akasha. The old energy of 'an eye-for-an-eye" on the other hand keeps our personal vibrations at their lowest and keeps us trapped in the past.

Forgiveness is an eternal virtue that holds the universe together.

All good comes from forgiveness. The human species continues life here and hereafter because of God's ultimate forgiveness and thus forgiveness, though not easy, is duly recompensed as a holy act. Forgiveness, not punishment, is the might of those who are truly mighty, and forgiveness and gentleness are the qualities of the self-possessed.

27. The Law of Free Will

The goal of the ascendant being is to voluntarily and willingly surrender the ego, hanging up the Soul-Overcoat of manifestation in order to become a perfected spirit regardless of how many lifetimes it takes. However, each of us in this regard has free will and free choice. We have the power to choose our direction—towards or away from the universal light and harmony—no matter what our circumstances, just as we choose to be under the power of others or an example to others.

The mind builds the thoughts that influence our choices manifest in the hundreds of actions and reactions that lead us to the circumstances we find ourselves in today. Our choices influence our experience, and our experience again influences our minds. It is a cycle, but whether a vicious cycle or not depends largely on the choices we make. Just as Adam and Eve had the choice to eat of the forbidden fruit, and even as their choice affected human experience irrevocably and forever, we face choices daily that only seem to be of less consequence. They are, in fact, tantamount. These "small choices" determine whether we live in the darkness or the light.

We in third dimension have the right to expand or contract, to bring our creative and expressive energies out into the world in positive or negative ways. This is our ultimate decision. The free will we use to create our choices mixes with our ability to love profoundly, and therefore the law of free will determines the amount of time we will spend in the attempt to merge with the Great Soul of all Creation.

28. The Law of Gender

All life forms contain the two elements of gender—masculine and feminine—yin and yang. On the great physical plane, the sexes of all species are manifested as male and female. On the great mental plane, gender manifests as masculine and feminine energies that exist within each and every person. Every male has its female element, and every female has its male element. On the great spiritual plane, gender manifests as the Father-Mother principle of the Infinite Omnipresent God in whose mind the universe is conceived and firmly held. It is written, "We all live, move, and have our being within God." When balance and learning reach a critical mass, the personality achieves the merger with God, and we see self as neither male nor female, but as one blended self.

This law embodies the Truth that gender is manifested in everything; masculine and feminine are ever at work on all planes of causation, just surely as protons (+) and electrons (-) are constantly at work in the atom. Gender manifests on all three planes of causation which are the great spiritual plane, the great mental plane, and the great physical plane. The law is always the same on all planes, but on the higher planes, it takes higher forms of manifestation. This law works in the direction of generation, regeneration, and creation.

29. The Law of Good Will

The will-to-good of the world knowers is the magnetic seed of the future." Our mental capacity today readily connects to those universal ideas which constitute the purpose behind the form. We each have the ability to mentally construct a happening, and see it through to completion. This is the "will-to-good." The will-to-good is always an education process where the recipients are left free to receive the idea or not. The responsibility for expanding the amount of goodwill in the world rests directly on the shoulders of the intelligentsia of the world. In the goodwill process it is the creative/idea/problem solving individuals who are directly responsible for creating goodwill.

In an energy relationship there is always a positive, creating side and a negative, receiving side of that creative relation. This is simply how the world works. The will-to-good is the positive, creative impetus, which, when received, makes the manifestation of goodwill possible. We are either mentally polarized or emotionally polarized. However, only those who are mentally polarized can begin to appropriate this energy through will on the mental plane. When this is fully comprehended, we begin to realize why the manifestation of goodwill is not more widespread.

30. The Law of Grace

No sincere effort goes unnoticed, and the Law of Grace allows those who truly seek the greater good special dispensation: the Law of Karma may be waived to the diligent and loving earthhealer who works in good faith but forgets to put change in her parking meter. The Law of Grace intervenes, when needed and appropriate, to allow us a dispensation from any negative consequences of a karma incurrence and it ensures we do not interfere with another's soul plan.

To benefit from the law of grace requires that we live in grace and that our efforts are sincere. It cannot be abused or it disappears leaving the would-be user with the repercussions—a fall from grace as it were.

Those who by virtue of their endeavours and service to others merit occasional graceful intervention can invoke the law simply by inserting in the request, "Under the Law of Grace…"

31. The Law of Group Endeavour

There is power in numbers. Whenever like-minded individuals come together to pray, manifest, do light-work, or even to create degrees of control we define as evil or black magic, their power is multiplied. Where the efforts of an individual may equal one unit, the efforts of two praying or healing for a common goal with equal energy will affect the energy of twenty units instead of the sum total of two. With three, the resultant energy explodes further.

The Law of Group Endeavour defines the multiplying of energy created when like minds and like hearts work in unison.

32. The Law of Group Life

No being exists in isolation; the choices we manifest in our thoughts are but one thread in the infinite tapestry of life, a small part of a whole that includes the rest of humanity. We must, then, look beyond ourselves, our families, and even our communities and nations to think in terms of the greater good of the universe itself. Fairness and fair play are universal, and the initiate cannot seek benefit to self that results in a detriment to the "group" or any of the individuals that make it up. This is the Law of Brotherhood or the Law of Group Life. We must consider our actions and our thoughts in light of universal questions: Is it the truth (for everyone, not just one group or individual)? Is it fair to all involved? Will it be of benefit to all?

Practice makes perfect, and with practice, thinking and acting within the group context and in the groups best interests will gradually become part of our collective consciousness. As civilization adjusts itself to these new conditions self-aggrandizement ceases to be the sole focus of governments and individuals. All aspects of life are interdependent, and when one proceeds to fuller, more universal thinking all of the group, including the original thinker benefit in manifold.

33. The Law of Healing

"We are but the hands of God, here to do His work." Hands-on healers, whose brain waves reverberate the Earth's pulse (7.8 Hz) channel energy to remove blockages or instil the sacred energy to the past, present or future. The Law of Healing also enables us to heal ourselves in the third dimension by virtue of a leap of faith: the faith that we are already healed.

34. The Law of Higher Will

When we surrender our smaller self and will to the guidance of a higher will and dedicate our actions for the highest good of ALL concerned, we feel an inspired glow at the centre of our lives. It is this feeling that enables us to move beyond our separate selves and smaller wills to relinquish control to the Higher Will whose knowledge and wisdom is infinitely greater than our own.

35. The Law of Honesty

Whether we like it or not, we tend to be self-cantered and we tend to act in our own best interests. If we have to lie to ourselves to do so we are likely to be surprised how gullible we are when it comes to accepting a 'convenient lie'.

Only when we are completely honest with ourselves about ourselves can we speak or act honestly with others. Furthermore, integrity and honesty require that we go beyond thought to act in line with higher laws despite strong impulses to the contrary. These impulses are but the yipping of latent self-interest.

Fear is no excuse. When we let fear stop us from expressing our true feelings and needs, we are being dishonest with ourselves and it costs us a sense of energy and spirit.

There is no punishment for acting in contravention of spiritual and higher laws such as the Law of Honesty. Breaking the law is its own punishment as it changes vibrational levels of our spirit energy and sets into motion subtle forces whose natural consequences we cannot escape any more than we can escape the force of gravity.

36. The Law of Identity

Inherent in the Law of Identity is the unique right each of us has to create our own identity. This is often called "being-ness". Our identity spans "lifetimes" and includes time between incarnations as well as third-dimensional incarnational experiences. Furthermore, identity does not cease when an entity merges with the Great Centre, as we may again separate to accomplish a goal in our former individual identity.

37. The Law of Intention

"Words without deeds are dead," we are told, and the same holds true for thoughts. Energy must follow intention or that which is perceived will not take place. All that holds us back from action in a worthy cause—fear, sloth, selfishness and so forth—constitutes bad intent.

The Law of Intention also speaks to motives. When we speak to "sound good" but fail to follow through, just as when we act but act for purposes of recognition or self-benefit our motives and our energy are skewed. No good can come of poor intentions. Intention and effort must be sincere (of higher vibration) to achieve genuine spiritual growth or reward.

38. The Law of Intuition

We can only know and act on our own intuition and inner wisdom when we trust our inner selves and feelings over the dictates and authority of others. We must trust and value our own intuition and have a sense of our own identity in order to hear our inner voices over the clamour of the crowd. When we know ourselves, we hear ourselves. Our intuition becomes more profound when have claimed our own sacred identity.

39. The Law of Justice

Justice rings to the farthest reaches of the known universe and beyond. Those who are just have banished forever all thwarting crosscurrents of ego. Those who are unjust will find no place to hide. The Law of Justice is instantaneous and when violated the universe conspires for retribution. This we know as karma.

40. The Law of Karma

Every cause has its' effect; every effect has its cause. Chance is but a name for law not recognized. There are many planes of causation, but nothing escapes the law. It is ever at work with chains of causations and effects that govern all of life and manifested matter.

The karmic law requires that every human wish find ultimate fulfilment. Therefore, desire is the chain that binds man to the reincarnation wheel. Karma is attracted only where the magnet of the personal ego still exists. An understanding of karma as the law of justice underlying life's inequalities serves to free the human mind from resentment against God and man.

The law itself is illusive and cannot be proven other than observed with the mind and is used to determine the causations and effects of specific events. When this law is used with conscious effort, desired results can be produced in a person's life. These effects steer us along definite paths of causation. When the law is used by an unconscious and haphazard mind, the effects are potentially disastrous for the individual or group of individuals. So called "accidents" could occur without warning to individuals who toil through life without awareness.

Because there are seven dimensions of reality in which causations can occur, we remain unaware of many reasons for effects. By understanding Universal laws we can learn to operate in grace instead of accumulating karma. This law is mechanically or mathematically operative; its workings may be scientifically manipulated by men and women of divine wisdom who are fully realized.

Karma can be understood to the observing mind which sees the cycles in all things, and realizes that all things follow the Great Law. We are responsible for the very thoughts that we produce are the final result of our own mental alchemy. In every minute thought, action, and deed that is performed, we set into motion unseen chains of causation and effect which will vibrate from the mental plane throughout the entire cellular structure of body, out into the environment, and finally into the cosmos. Eventually the vibratory energy returns to its originator upon the return swing of the pendulum. And all this takes less time than the twinkling of an eye.

41. The Law of Knowledge

Knowledge is energy that can be applied, used or misused. As the consequences of misuse can be dire, much information is withheld from initiates. It is not until the initiate achieves the knowledge and status of the pledged disciple that more will be revealed.

In-depth knowledge is not required for the initiate to progress to higher levels. All that is required is: 1) the right apprehension of energy: its sources, qualities, types and vibrations and 2) the right apprehension of the laws of energy and conservation of force. The Law of Knowledge dictates that due knowledge shall arrive to the seeker in due time.

42. The Law of Love

To understand love we must differentiate between love that is desire—love in the personality, love that is magnetic and love that is transformative. Each phase marks a period of completion; each is a starting point for fresh endeavours in life. Thus the soul migrates from the personality and back again to its source. From this perspective we see that there is a vast difference between love and desire which limits love.

43. The Law of Magnetic Control

Every thought we have creates a match that comes back to us like a boomerang, and in the development of the control of this law lies hidden the control of the personality by the Monad via the egoic body.

One of the seven laws of our solar system, under the three major laws, The Law of Magnetic Control dictates that our thoughts, especially thoughts on the Buddhic plane are charged with energy. Furthermore, like energies attract. Thus our thoughts are galvanized to their correlatives; every thought has the potential to grow. We see this in the principal of "the eleventh monkey" that posits that like thoughts combine until it requires only one more thought to galvanize them into a reality on the material plane.

44. The Law of Magnetic Impulse

Also known as the Law or Polar Union whose symbol is two fiery balls united by a triangle of fire, the Law of Magnetic Impulse is the manifesting factor and the first step towards universal union.

The Law of Magnetic Impulse results in an eventual union between the man and the group which produces harmonious group relations.

45. The Law of Magnetism

The Law of Magnetism speaks to the unifying of the personality. It is an expression of lunar force. The Law of Magnetism has three distinct phases: the stage of intellectuality or artistic attainment, the stage of discipleship, and the stage known as Treading the Path. By completing each of these stages we affect a synthesis and unify the energies commonly associated with attraction.

46. The Law of Manifestation

Although invisible, thought is a force just as electricity and gravitation are forces. The human mind is a spark of the almighty consciousness of God. Whatever the powerful mind (holding a pure thought - that which excludes any other thought) believes very intensely will instantly come to pass. There are actions, sounds, techniques, mental energy and symbols which when understood enable us to manifest energy (love, joy, peace, etc.) into our auras. With practice and increased love held in the heart and emotional body we are eventually able to manifest physical objects.

47. The Law of Mantras

Through the mantra we connect and become one with the Higher Being. Each mantra is linked to a certain manifestation of the absolute Divinity, and in true mantra practice, when we forget the self-chanting to become the mantra itself; we attain a state where nothing but the mantra exists.

Thus we connect. The mantra represents the name of a Master Being and connects us to the ray of light emanating from that being. We connect through the sounds "aum," 'om," "hu," etc. with a resonance and frequency that is profoundly beneficial in raising the vibration of the self.

48. The Law of Meditation

This is the law of current or unified thought that is a continuum of mental effort aimed at assimilating the object of meditation. It is free from any other thought. Time does not exist and what we refer to as past and future have no bearing on the mental plane. Time becomes a convention of thought and language a social agreement. Truth lies in the moment—this moment—the only moment that actually exists. Anxiety about past and future only serve to maintain the anxiety, as the mental pictures we create then manifest in our lives. When we practice remembering that the here and now is all we have, our present moments improve.

49. The Law of Process

Enlightenment is a process, not an event. Whether we reach nirvana within this reincarnation cycle or not, meditating calms the inner self. At its most profound the Law of Process culminates in the merging with the God-source or "enlightenment" as the Buddhists would call it.

50. The Law of Mentalism

The mind is ALL. ALL is the mind. It is spirit indefinable, unknowable, and thought of as a universal, infinite, living mind. The ALL consists of all universal knowledge, the substantial reality underlying all the outward empirical manifestations. The material universe, phenomena, matter, energy and all that is apparent to our material senses is part of the ALL.

The Law of Mentalism explains the true nature of energy, power and matter. The Universe is mental in nature. The atom of matter, the unit of force, the mind of man, and the being of the arch-angel are all but degrees in one scale, and all fundamentally the same. The difference is solely a matter of degree and rate of vibration. All are creations of the All, and have their existence solely within the Infinite Mind of the All. Mental transmutation is the art of changing the conditions of the universe, along the lines of matter, force, and mind.

51. The Law of Miracles

All events in our precisely adjusted universe are lawfully wrought and lawfully explicable. The socalled miraculous powers of a great master are but the natural accompaniments to his or her exact understanding of subtle laws that operate in the inner cosmos of the consciousness. Nothing is a miracle, yet in the truest sense, everything is a miracle. Is anything more miraculous than that each of us is encased in an intricately organized body, and is set upon on earth whirling through space among the stars?

The Law of Miracles is operable by any person who has realized that the essence of creation is light. A master is able to employ his/her divine knowledge of light phenomena to project instantly into perceptible manifestation the ubiquitous light atoms. The actual form of the projection (whatever it is water into wine, medicine, a human body) is determined by the master's wish and limited only by his or her powers of will and visualization.

52. The Law of No Judgments

We are not judged, nor should we judge. The Universal Spirit does not judge, for judgments are human inventions: a means to compare, contrast, and above all, control as we measure ourselves and others against shallow and idealistic standards of perfection, morality and truth. Judgment attracts judgment, and under the Law of Equities: so as we judge, so shall we be judged. The only real assessment is that we conduct upon ourselves after death as a condition of living in the duality of the third dimension.

53. The Law of Non-Attachment

Enlightenment is non-attachment. The ultimate nature of the self is Empty. The self does not exist as a separate entity. Attachment to the self creates karma. Non-attachment to the self dissolves karma.

A full conceptual understanding needs to occur, as mere conceptual understanding that the self is empty and, hence, detached does not lead to liberation. Many methods have been devised to help human beings attain this realization. These usually fall into two categories. The first is 'nonattached behaviour' and the other is called 'spiritual practice.' Through diligent application of these methods, an individual can free him or herself from the confines of judgment to achieve that which is real and attainable, his true karma-determined existence.

54. The Law of Non-Intervention

The karma repercussions of intervention are dire, indeed. The Law of Non-intervention dictates that no spirit is allowed to channel material to a recipient that would force a change in the evolution of that person. Although we can accept intervention from another source by going into a trance and allowing our consciousness to leave for another to enter and impart knowledge, we cannot force our knowledge or interventions on others.

The Law of Non-intervention concerns the individual and group right to serve self rather than to live in the vibration of service to others. This law prevents physical and non-physical beings from intervening to correct what they see as wrong or harmful in others, as doing so would rob them of the chance to auto-correct and address their karma in the process.

55. The Law of One

The universe is ONE. The Lord is ONE. All that is, was, and will be has its being in the ONE. So it is with life. So it is with consciousness. The enlightened being lives within the ONENESS of that Universal Consciousness on Earth.

56. The Law of Order of Creation

Creation is yin and yang, darkness and light. All that exists is conceived in spirit and grows in the light of the mental plane before it is manifested in the material. All begins as light. However, the children of God and the Children of Men direct and force the light into channels for power, turning it into a destructive, dark force. Whereas man has leaned towards the dark for many centuries, the balance of light and dark is shifting. We are now reaching the turning point where the light shall exceed the darkness.

57. The Law of Patience

Every soul is unique and each will come to its enlightenment in its own time. We cannot force that onto the being which is not YET meant to be. Through Patience we know ourselves; we test our ideals and realize that the faults we find in others are faults we know from prior experience. Patiently we seek true understanding. As Luke says, "In your patience possess ye your souls."

Patience requires spiritual, mental, and physical thought and action, and through patience we learn faith and understanding. Patience allows all other virtues to manifest more profoundly, proportional to the patience we exercise in the process.

58. The Law of Patterns

Our ability to make change is largely dictated by the ways we learn when we are young. We learn to make sense of the world by observing patterns, and this has survival value. However, patterns quickly transform into habits, both good and bad.

We can reward good habits in due proportion while retaining our spontaneity: we can be open to positive change, to doing old things in new ways and to restructuring our lives and our behaviours to achieve positive growth. We can and should examine our patterns and correct those we find dysfunctional, negative, or destructive. "Every action has an equal and opposite reaction," and any habit or pattern, whether we call it good or bad, tends to reassert itself over time unless we break that pattern by doing something different—something that will have enough impact to interrupt the old pattern.

59. The Law of Perfection

From a transcendental perspective, everyone and everything is unconditionally perfect. From a conventional viewpoint, perfection does not exist. Excellence is the best we can achieve, and achieving it takes time and practice. However, although perfection itself may be difficult to obtain, The Law of Perfection speaks to the perfectness of our unfolding. Despite wrong turns and ups and downs, our journey towards perfection is perfect in itself if we are in tune with the universal spirit and our karma. As long as we are "unfolding" we are progressing "perfectly." When we understand the larger picture, we understand our role and responsibility in helping the world we live in to become more loving, giving, kinder and gentler, we live up to this responsibility and expand into the perfection of our higher selves.

60. The Law of Periodicity

Rhythm, ebb and flow, are the measured beat of the pulsating life and the law of the universe. In learning to respond to the vibration of the high Places, this rhythmic periodicity must be borne in mind. Training for the aspirant will by cyclic, and will have its ebb and flow, as all else in nature. Times of activity are followed by times of pralaya, and periods of registered contact alternate with periods of apparent silence. If the student develops as desired, each pralayic period is succeeded by one of greater activity, and of more potent achievement.

61. The Law of Polarity

Everything is dual. Everything is polarized. Like and unlike are but two sides of the same coin.Opposites are different in degree but identical in nature. All paradoxes can be reconciled within the whole. Without the law of polarity - light, gravity and electricity would not be possible.

The law of cause and effect is closely connected to polarity and holds us true to the choices we make and the actions we take by returning to us what we have measured out to others. Like the swing of the pendulum, our energy always returns where it began. In biblical terms it is expressed as, "Whatsoever a man sows, so shall he reap" and "Do unto others, as you would have them to you."

The evidence of this principle is observed in the polarity of planets and the various celestial bodies that include our earth, solar system, and galaxy. On the mental plane, this principle manifests itself in the heart-centre of each person as the enlightened mind. The Principle of Polarity makes possible the choices we make on the scale of life between good and evil, right and wrong, generosity and greed, love and fear, truth and lies.

The law of cause and effect is closely connected to polarity and holds us true to the choices and actions we make by returning to us what we have measured out to others. Like the swing of the pendulum, it always returns where it began.

62. The Law of the Present Moment

We must all be aware that we have goals—things seemingly great and small to accomplish within our lives. Whether our goals are small or large is of little consequence. Even the most daunting achievement can be managed in increments or "baby steps."

At the same time, the Law of the Present Moment tells us that there are no shortcuts. If we skip a single step the results are likely to be a failure. Skipping steps is a sure sign of impatience with the process. Instead, we must learn to appreciate and live in the moment. Big or small, the step we are taking NOW is the only step in the present moment, hence the only step that matters.

63. The Law of Progress

The universe is in a state of constant growth, and progress can be made in all directions; flux is at the heart of progress. We can progress in the pathways of good or evil. The informing consciousness is also in a constant state of change, and this informing consciousness is seen in the deva kingdom and in certain pranic energies. The Law of Progress dictates that what is needful will come into being.

64. The Law of Prophecy

The future is happening, unfolding in the "I AM." We are perpetually in the state of "NOW." The only true future that exists is the desire or will of the Source of all Creation that none shall be lost.

Sacred geometry is a manifestation of God's love. People who are able to tune into the Akashic records and the Universal Consciousness sometimes map a line from the supposed past to the present and then to the future. The ability to use sacred geometry comes with the raising of vibration to such a degree that the personality gains the right to assess Akasha for the good of another or of self.

When reading the energy going to the future of people on earth we must keep in mind, however, that energy changes from moment to moment. While those powerful prophets of old were correct in their time and some of what they said has held true to present day, many of their prophecies have lost relevancy. The Law of Prophecy suggests we be sceptical of prophecy due to the complex and ever changing nature of the universe. Furthermore, just by hearing prediction, we change the outcome to some degree, thus rendering our 'prophecy' automatically irrelevant.

65. The Law of Radiation

Liberation means the ability of any conscious atom to pass out of one sphere of energized influence into another of a higher vibration and thus manifesting a larger and wider expanse of conscious realization.

Understanding the radiatory or emancipatory condition of all substances as a specific point in evolution allows us to approach Reality. The Law of Radiation governs the outer effect produced by all forms in all kingdoms. When their internal activity has reached such a stage of vibratory activity that the confining walls of the form no longer form a prison, the Law of Radiation permits the liberation of the subjective essence. Liberation means the ability of any conscious atom to pass out of one sphere of energized influence into another sphere of a higher vibration and a larger and wider expanse of conscious realization.

66. The Law of Rebirth

This law, when understood, will do much to solve the problems of sex and marriage for those who understand the true nature of life-as-continuum tread more carefully down its paths. Those who understand the Law of Rebirth know that each life represents a mass of ancient obligations requiring the recovery of old relations. Each evolving soul seeks the opportunity to pay old debts, a chance to make restitution and progress. This often requires the awakening of deep-seated qualities, the recognition of old friends and enemies, the solution of revolting injustices and the understanding of that which conditions the man and makes him what he is.

67. The Law of Rebound

The Law of Rebound enables us to come out of negative situations stronger, wiser, and bolder. If we do not gain a clear victory or even if we are utterly defeated, the soul grows in the process. We have seen this in stories since the beginning of mankind. The initiate who understands the Law of Rebound may lose the battle, but still win the war. By trying we build wisdom and resilience that will stand us in good stead, even if we fail. Traumatic situations often create the need for rebound, and the soul sees in these negative occurrences of the opportunity to give self and others to affect a leap in faith.

68. The Law of Responsibility

Acting responsibly requires that we establish the limits and boundaries of our responsibility, taking full charge of that which is our duty and letting go of that which is not. We find more enjoyment supporting others as we create more harmonious co-operative relationships by understanding and focusing exclusively on that which falls within our realm of responsibility. Under this law we understand the need to over co-operate but NOT to the extent that we becomes co-dependent - the condition characterized by an obsessive focus on other people's lives. This law reminds us to respect our internal values and find our own point of balance.

69. The Law of Rhythm

The Law of Rhythm the most visible of all principles on the physical plane. Its power is reflected within the forces of nature which move the waves and tides of our oceans and cause the continuous changes of the seasons. The Law of Rhythm is observed in the continuous cycles of life and death, and in the rebirth of all things including the rise and fall of governments and nations and the constant creation and destruction of suns, worlds, and galaxies. Everything flows, out and in; everything has its "tides;" all things rise and fall; the pendulum-swing manifests in everything, and the measure of the swing to the right is the measure of the swing to the left; rhythm compensates.

Rhythm is the law of compensation and The Law of Rhythm maintains equilibrium in all things. It returns to us that which we give out in life. The return swing of the pendulum is assured without fail and there is no escape from the effects of this immutable law. The door of universal law swings in all directions. The final result depends what we have chosen to believe and whether or not our belief system allows us to see the truth as it really is. If we do not want to know the truth or do not care, we will evolve through the standard process of evolution. Nothing can, or is allowed to stand still.

All manifestation is the result of active energy producing certain results, and expenditure of energy in any one direction will necessitate an equal expenditure in an opposite direction.

This law holds us true to what we believe and compensates us accordingly. The pendulum-like swing of rhythm is immutable and we can only counteract its backward swing by mentally polarizing ourselves in a desirable position on the scale of life. It requires a dedicated personal commitment to cultivate the unknown within all of us in order to cause a quantum leap in the evolutionary process of life with all its aches and pains. This is a mental art that is known to hierophants, adepts, and masters of all ages. We will fulfil the Law of Rhythm one way or another, either by using the law to our advantage or by become its subject.

70. The Law of Right Human Relations

No man, or woman for that matter, is a prophet. No one has a franchise on reality; no one knows "the best way to do things." No one, then, can dictate to another. "Let no one assume to forcibly teach, counsel or guide, for we all have the greatest of these we could hope for already within us." The only being we can really counsel is the self. In our relationships we achieve greater results with others by our own fine example and by listening. People answer their own questions if given the opportunity. The only real control we ever have and need is the control of self.

And yet, there are those for whom teaching is a means to an end, be that control, self-avoidance or self-aggrandizement. These pseudo-teachers have no students—only victims. A strong action may be required to thwart such a teacher and become independent of another's will. The Law of Right Human Relations recognizes this right. We are all pupils and learners in the third dimension. By diverting our attentions to others and failing to search for excellence within, we lose sight of the gifts we already have, overlooking them in our haste to teach others.

71. The Law of Schools
(The Law of Love & Light)

As initiates who have transcended the stage of self-consciousness we are governed by the Law of Schools, also known as the Law of Love and Light. The consciousness does not expand helterskelter. As initiates we must undergo a transformation of consciousness including knowledge of the Higher Self required to produce alignment and illumination; the knowledge of our Guru or that which we seek to know; knowledge of the tools needed to conduct our work and service; and finally, knowledge of other souls with whom we can work. The Law of Schools is a mysterious term used to cover universal law as it affects the expansion of consciousness initiates undergo.

72. The Law of Service

The Law of Service grows naturally out of the successful application of the sciences of the antahkarana and meditation. It is the governing law of the future. Growth is achieved by forgetting self in the service of the race. With the linking of soul and personality the light of the soul pours into the brain consciousness, resulting in the subordination of the lower to the higher. This identification produces a corresponding activity in the personal life and an outpouring of the activity we call service. If the evasion of this law is a conscious action, there are karmic penalties. This work requires sacrifice of time and personal interest; it requires deliberate effort, conscious wisdom and the ability to work without attachment.

73. The Law of Solar Evolution

This law, the sum total of all the lesser Solar laws and activities is more properly subject matter for those who have moved beyond the initiate stage. They are too numerous to summarize here.

74. The Law of Sound

The release of energy in the atom is linked to the science of sound, meaning that every living thing in existence has a sound. Through knowledge of these sounds we can bring about change and evolve new forms of knowledge.

Healing with sound has proved effective as sound has the capacity to restore us to our harmonic patterns. Chanting, tuning forks, and music can all bring about great healing and change. This is enhanced geometrically by the Law of the Group. Chanting with a group heightens the effect of the mantra. The most powerful mantra presently known to man is the Dali Lama's favourite "Om mani padme hum," six syllables thought to be capable of purifying the six realms of existence.

75. The Law of Spiritual Approach

It is the goal of every conscious being to become a walking, talking example of the God-self. The Law of Spiritual Approach shows us that behind our every thought, word, action, and prayer is the Creator of All. When we learn to approach this spiritual being, we learn the correct spiritual approach for all situations and all beings: one of deference in respect. When we approach others and the Creator appropriately, our personalities become the reflection of the god-self for others to learn from and emulate. This is how we become our higher and better selves.

76. The Law of Spiritual Awakening

A basic level of self-control and stability is required to maintain the degree of effort required for the awakening of other states of awareness. Because such awakening brings with it higher forms of perception and power, self-centred misuse of the greater perception and power bears a proportionally graver karmic consequence. Spiritual Awakening brings with it the need for moral impeccability.

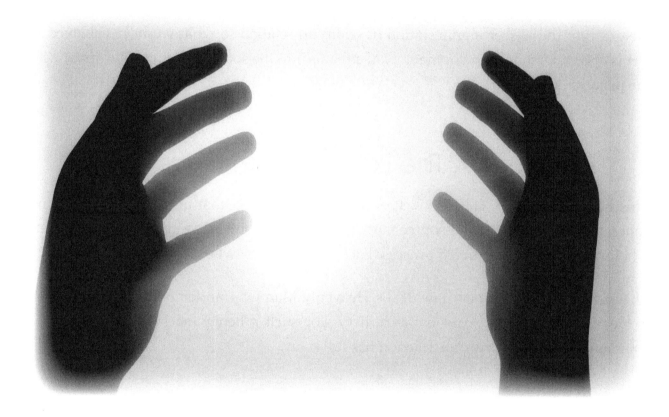

77. The Law of Summons

Through "soul-talk" and the Law of Summons we can learn how to relinquish the soul from the physical body and summon another soul with whom to have a soul-to-soul talk. The Law of Summons is one of the most powerful laws and requires that there be no conscious ego involved. Only thus can the message of love or the explanation of events from the perspective of a different soul be accepted profoundly in the manner it is intended.

78. The Law of Surrender

Until we have attained complete trust and faith in God we are likely to view surrender as a leap into the abyss or as death. Because we so cherish the self, relinquishing the ego is a very frightening experience. When we have absolute faith and trust, we accept that the self, once abandoned, merges with a higher stage of existence which is ready, willing and waiting for it. This is the "white light" of the next plane of existence near-death survivors see. It is the light of enlightenment and the white lotus flower that represents the unfolding of the universe as we merge with the God-light. At the time of surrender our entire being merges into the higher manifestation of reality in relation to what we have achieved in terms of our personal development. God streams into the soul that has created space with the negation of the self.

79. The Law of Synthesis

This is the concept of THE ONE. It is founded in the fact that all things, abstract and concrete stem from the God-source, are "units" of His thought, and are thus a concrete whole and not a differentiated process. Each "piece" of the whole is the whole.

This paradox is the primary law of the Heavenly Man who understands that each piece is the whole, the centre and the periphery. For such a being the Law of Economy is transcended and the Law of Attraction has full sway.

80. The Law of Teaching

Our future depends entirely on whether we learn to adapt to new more positive and holistic ways of thinking consistent with the positive energy in the universe—or not. Only then will we change from the old, dark ways of domination to new worlds of independence and interdependence. Without teaching and the assistance of the Great Masters past and present, it is unlikely that enough of a shift towards the light to effect dramatic and lasting change will be generated. The Law of Teaching encourages us, then, to share what we know and just as importantly to learn from others.

81. The Law of Telepathy

Through telepathy the fine vibrations of thoughts in one person's mind are transmitted through the subtle vibrations of astral ether and then through the grosser earthly ether, creating electrical waves which, in turn, translate themselves into thought waves in the mind of another person. The "third eye" or point between the eyebrows is the apparatus whereby thoughts are broadcast. However, they are heard in the heart. When the feeling of calm is concentrated in the heart, our psychic hearing is at its best. The heart acts as a mental radio, receiving the messages of others from far or near.

82. The Law of Three Requests

Whoso doubts the power of three simply isn't paying attention. Three is the Trinity, the number of magic wishes we get in fairy tales, the number of little pigs whose sagacity and building skills were tested by the big, bad wolf, and, as we all know, "the third time's the charm." Similarly, whenever we pray or request a higher power to assist us and whenever we invoke the Law of Grace, we bring stronger energy to the effort by repeating our request or prayer three times.

83. The Law of Time

The only moment we have is now. This is our realm; the "now" is where we are and where we create. What we have done is past, and when any cycle is completed that moment in history exists only as a record or energy trace in time and space. Third dimension linear time is for those living under the veil of forgetfulness. It allows them to centre on the moment and a perceived sense of order so they can avoid the burdens that come with the remembrance of past lives.

The consequences of past actions are atoned through karma, and can be rewritten to a degree, but only in the NOW. The FUTURE consists of today's thoughts, dressed by emotion and driven by action.

Activity is the key. Time is more rigid in the third than in the fourth dimension, yet only the most consciously evolved are able to master time. There are those who can slip into 'no time' but these are people who have raised their personal vibration by demonstrating many virtues, dispensing a great deal of positive karma and by relinquishing the ego entirely. They have spent years and lifetimes amassing the information and skill to suspend time.

84. The Law of Unconditional Love

Loving ourselves and other people as they are is a form of honouring the soul path of the self and the other. Loving without judgment or reservation creates the awareness that we are all part of God or the All. When we love without condition or restraint we connect profoundly with our higher selves. When we love unconditionally we notice that we say the right things at the right time; we're where we need to be when we need to be there, and life and events seem to flow to us in a more joyous and agreeable manner. Everything seems easier when living in unconditional love.

85. The Law of Unity

We all bear the seed of Divinity within us and are thus all connected to one another. This is the way we start, and the way we develop into eternity. It is only while in third dimension physical form where we are separated from our higher selves that we experience the illusion that we stand alone. Fear enters our emotional body because of this illusion and begins to close off our connection to the Source. When we experience great soul growth, in some small but profound manner, all souls throughout the universe benefit. All substance in this Universe flows to us and through us. We are All.

86. The Law of Vibration

Nothing rests; everything moves; everything vibrates. This is the law of progress, of movement and of rotation. One of the seven laws of our solar system, under the three major laws, the Law of Vibration is the law of progress, movement, and rotation. This Principal explains the differences in manifestations of matter, energy, mind and spirit, showing how each results from varying degrees and rates of vibration.

All that exists is in constant vibration and motion. Atoms vibrate so rapidly that they seem motionless to the physical eye. At the other end of the scale are things that vibrate so slowly that they also appear to be motionless or non-existent. In between are the various vibrations of living entities which range from consciousness all the way down to the lowly dust particle. And there are things even lower then dust. If we were to follow the scale of life all the way down to the utmost regions of the negative pole into pure undifferentiated matter, we again find ourselves in the realm of spirit - the Alpha and the Omega. All that is, begins in spirit and ends in spirit.

87. The Law of Will of God

God is all good, and it is by reason of the Good that all other things exist. It is God's will that what is human should be divine, and therefore all creation pushes forth to the God Light. God's working has to do with things free from change and movement - things divine. The creators of our world carry out their work of form-building under this law.

88. The Law of Will Power

This law depicts the right and condition of each personality or soul extension to generate its own degree of will power. As individuals developing soul extensions differ in degrees of will power from one to another, other entities, extensions and soul family members may not always agree with our will. Others in the soul family and/or other incarnational personalities (friends) may feel that our drive to accomplish something is overwhelming or obsessive. However, The Law of Will Power dictates that this is a question each of us must answer on our own. Answers will vary depending on the conditions of our incarnational experience and the objective of our will. If they are honest answers, gainfully sought through meditation chances are they are the right answers for our condition in the here-and-now. The Law of Will Power consistently shows us the right conditions under which we can and should exert our will.

PRACTICAL ASSIGNMENTS

Practical Assignment 1

It is no accident that I chose 88 universal laws to impart to you in this book. This number represents the masters from the Angelic Kingdom. In calling upon the loving support of the angelic kingdom, and in aligning with the Law of Miracles, what miracles are you powerfully requesting arrive at this moment in time in the most joyous, easy, miraculous way beyond what you ever could have hoped for or imagined.

List out the miracles that you are divinely commanding for your physical body, your mental and emotional body, your relationships (including yourself, your vocation and any other miracles that you would like to request at this time.)

Invoke the Law of Threes once you have completed your written request by writing, "thank you, amen, and so it is!"

Practical Assignment 2

I am a firm believer in the divine formula of aligned thought + aligned action = aligned results. If you applied this formula to the area of your life that does not seem to be manifesting as quickly as you would like, what is revealing itself in regards to the action that you need to take in order to consciously co-create the "and better"?

Set the intention that you are aligning with the Law of Action, call forward the wisdom of the 3 small, divinely aligned actions that you can take right now and write those down. Then, write out all of the things that will change (including how you feel) once these actions yields the results that you desire.

Practical Assignment 3

Create sacred time to list out the 3 Universal Laws that you feel most misaligned with. Write out what you are learning and how you are growing as a result of this 'misalignment'.

Then write out what you need to release (on an inner and outer level) in order to create greater alignment.

Lastly, write out who you need to become and what you need to call in to your life to create greater alignment with these laws.

Practical Assignment 4

Create sacred time to list out the Universal Laws that you feel most aligned with. Now, reflect on the wisdom that you have to share with others as a result of this alignment and write this down.

Then write out all of the people (groups or individuals) that can benefit most from this wisdom and create a plan of how you can reach them.

Practical Assignment 5

Create sacred space so that you can go inside and have a heart to heart with yourself about where you could benefit from taking action (i.e. your home, your career/business, your relationships, your health, etc.). Then tune in and write down below one small, next step action that you can take in each area to move your forward, when you will complete it, and how it will feel when you move forward on it.

Once complete, journal how it felt to complete the next steps, and then wash, rinse, repeat.

Practical Assignment 6

Take a moment to reflect on an inner conflict that you are having or a past or present conflict that you are experiencing with another person (i.e.. friend, parent, lover, etc). Go inside, set the intention that you are aligning with the Universal Law of Unconditional Love, and ask what will occur if you infuse that 'conflict' with the aligned wisdom of this law for the next 7 days.

Then, set aside a few moments each day to journal about what thoughts, memories, feelings and or shifts that you are noticing in regards to the conflict for the next days.

THANK YOU!

Thank you for taking this journey with me through some very powerful Universal Laws. If you would like to take your journey with me even further, be sure to visit http://www.souljourneys.ca/store/ to receive even more miracle-rich programs designed to support you on your soul's path.

ABOUT THE AUTHOR

Jennifer Longmore - 3 Time Best-Selling Author

Jennifer Longmore, North America's Soul Purpose Expert, internationally acclaimed host of "Soul Purpose Central," and best-selling author, is world-renowned for her laser like clarity in seeing into the depths of your soul and bridging your connection to universal consciousness. She is a leading expert on Akashic Records and has served thousands of souls as founder of the Soul Journeys® School for Akashic Studies and the Soul Journeys® Method.

For more than 15 years, she has served clients, just like you, in permanently shifting the limiting beliefs and patterns that prevent you from being who you really are so that you can live your most abundant, aligned, and accelerated soul's journey. With over 20,000 soul purpose sessions, including the who's-who of actors, professional athletes, CEO's of leading companies, and other influential luminaries, Jennifer continues to offer these high-level sessions to soul's who are really committed to shine their light.

For more information:

Web Site
SoulJourneys.ca

Social Media
Facebook - facebook.com/SoulPurposeExpert
Twitter - twitter.com/jenlongmore
LinkedIn - linkedin.com/in/soulpurposeexpert

Table of Contents

INTRODUCTION 7

1. The Law of Abundance 8
2. The Law of Action 9
3. The Law of Akasha 9
4. The Law of Analogy 10
5. The Law of Ascension 10
6. The Law of Attraction 11
7. The Law of Balance 12
8. The Law of Challenge 12
9. The Law of Cohesion 12
10. The Law of Colour 13
11. The Law of Common Ground 13
12. The Law of Consciousness 13
13. The Law of Continuity of Consciousness 14
14. The Law of Cycles 14
15. The Law of Divine Invocation 15
16. The Law of Discipline 15
17. The Law of Divine Flow 16
18. The Law of Divine Love and Oneness 17
19. The Law of Economy 17
20. The Law of Economy of Force 17
21. The Law of Equalities *(or Analogy)* 18
22. The Law of Expansion 19
23. The Law of Expectation 19
24. The Law of Faith 19
25. The Law of Flexibility 20
26. The Law of Forgiveness 21
27. The Law of Free Will 22

88 UNIVERSAL LAWS

28. The Law of Gender 22
29. The Law of Good Will 23
30. The Law of Grace 24
31. The Law of Group Endeavour 24
32. The Law of Group Life 25
33. The Law of Healing 26
34. The Law of Higher Will 26
35. The Law of Honesty 27
36. The Law of Identity 27
37. The Law of Intention 28
38. The Law of Intuition 28
39. The Law of Justice 28
40. The Law of Karma 29
41. The Law of Knowledge 30
42. The Law of Love 30
43. The Law of Magnetic Control 31
44. The Law of Magnetic Impulse 31
45. The Law of Magnetism 31
46. The Law of Manifestation 32
47. The Law of Mantras 32
48. The Law of Meditation 32
49. The Law of Process 33
50. The Law of Mentalism 33
51. The Law of Miracles 33
52. The Law of No Judgments 34
53. The Law of Non-Attachment 34
54. The Law of Non-Intervention 35
55. The Law of One 35
56. The Law of Order of Creation 36
57. The Law of Patience 36
58. The Law of Patterns 36
59. The Law of Perfection 37

88 UNIVERSAL LAWS

60. The Law of Periodicity 38
61. The Law of Polarity 38
62. The Law of the Present Moment 39
63. The Law of Progress 39
64. The Law of Prophecy 39
65. The Law of Radiation 40
66. The Law of Rebirth 40
67. The Law of Rebound 41
68. The Law of Responsibility 41
69. The Law of Rhythm 41
70. The Law of Right Human Relations 42
71. The Law of Schools *(The Law of Love & Light)* 43
72. The Law of Service 43
73. The Law of Solar Evolution 44
74. The Law of Sound 44
75. The Law of Spiritual Approach 44
76. The Law of Spiritual Awakening 45
77. The Law of Summons 45
78. The Law of Surrender 46
79. The Law of Synthesis 46
80. The Law of Teaching 46
81. The Law of Telepathy 47
82. The Law of Three Requests 47
83. The Law of Time 48
84. The Law of Unconditional Love 48
85. The Law of Unity 49
86. The Law of Vibration 49
87. The Law of Will of God 49
88. The Law of Will Power 50

PRACTICAL ASSIGNMENTS 51
ABOUT THE AUTHOR 59

88 UNIVERSAL LAWS

INTRODUCTION

All creation is governed by laws - universal principles, if you will. The principles that operate in the outer universe, discoverable by scientists, are called natural laws. Some we can see, like the orbit of the stars and the changing of the seasons, while others, like gravity are invisible but exist beyond a doubt. We are energy, and what we say, think and do creates energy around us.

And there are subtler laws that rule the hidden spiritual planes and the inner realms of consciousness. Contained within these laws (or conditions) is the true nature of matter.

Knowledge of the laws that govern everything in the universe from the mighty cosmos to the tiny atom affects how you think, how you relate to the universe and others in it, and how the universe and others in it relate to you.

Love is the foundation of universal law: the mind the builder of your universe. The mind that is fully aware and attuned to the application of universal law in all matters is the mind that knows that in love all life is given, in love all things move.

Every action has an equal and opposite reaction. Every yin has its yang. Thus, in giving one attains. In giving one acquires. In giving, love becomes the fulfillment of desire, guided and directed in the ways that bring the more perfect knowledge of self as related to the universal, all powerful, all guiding, all divine influence in life. Love IS life. To give IS to receive.

When we go back, merge with the God Source, in some infinitesimal but profound way, we expand the Mind of God.

Our God is manifest in our and higher selves and always points to the best and most perfect way. It is ours to listen and accept or reject what we hear. God does not blame, but patiently tries again to show the perfect way, the loving way. All of creation pushes forth. – As we listen we are ever becoming. Identity ever remains!

1. The Law of Abundance

Why do some people seem to 'come up smelling like roses' regardless what happens to them? Why do others who make more effort make less progress in achieving their goals?

Also known as the Law of Opulence and the Law of Success, the Law of Abundance speaks to all we have in our lives on the inner and outer, social, emotional, and spiritual levels.

The law of abundance reveals that our wishes do come true, whether we wish poorly or we wish well. It does not apply only to money and material well-being, for indeed, there are many kinds of wealth and abundance manifests itself in many ways. The man who looks proudly on his children is wealthy, as is the woman who doesn't 'have it all' but is truly happy with who she is and 'all she has'.

We can have a wealth of common sense, understanding, and kindness. Or we can have the opposite. The choice is ours. We can manifest the wealth we want in our lives, but we must be mindful that we are much more than the sum-total of our possessions. When creating the abundance of financial gain we must remember to be IN this world, but not OF this world.

2. The Law of Action

No matter how strongly we feel what we feel or how much faith we have in what we know, feelings and knowledge are fruitless unless we act upon them. We may understand concepts such as commitment, courage, and love, but we do not know them until we act. Knowledge is action; doing becomes understanding. Our gifts and talents are only latent possibilities until we bring them to life.

Every aspirant is the focal point of energy in the midst of a whirlwind of energy, the chaos of the third dimension. Every aspirant must make his or her presence felt through action.

The universe responds to action. When we take deliberate action on behalf of something that we wish to create/change/shift, the universe observes this as readiness, and then brings you what you have now demonstrated you can handle. Remember: the universe *never* gives you what you can't handle!

3. The Law of Akasha

Akasha, the fifth and quintessential element, is the unifying force of the universe manifested in the intelligence of substance. Everything in the universe operates within the realm of unerring law because everything emanates from the same source energy. We are all 'one spirit' and all part and parcel of the cosmos, subject to the law of Akasha. The individual who lives in harmony with the universal force 'goes with the flow,' and all things prosper for she is riding the wave of creation.

In humans, Akasha refers to our ethereal spirit-being that cannot be seen but truly defines us as individuals. It is our interaction with the universal spirit, whether we tend it or neglect it, not 'life' or 'luck' that ultimately determines our fate.

4. The Law of Analogy

How is the universe like a hurricane? The energy infusing the universe manifests itself at every level in a multitude of different but analogous ways, and these analogies can be used to further understanding at all levels. The sweeping arc of the universe pictured from afar is 'the same' as the sweeping arc of a hurricane bearing down on land. An emotional storm in life is a whirlwind of violent emotion often called a 'perfect storm' or a 'hurricane'.

No analogy is ever exact as energy adapts itself to the moment, yet analogies enable us to explain the unexplainable by means of comparisons and this enables us to convey understanding in a broad sense.

5. The Law of Ascension

Think of yourself as a single string on a guitar. The other strings are the energy beings you attract, making up your life - the whole guitar. When strummed, whether poorly or well, each string resonates energy in the form of sound just as energy resonates from the soul of an incarnational being.

Those who are 'in tune' with universal energy and have lost the illusion that they are separated from the god-self, and they vibrate in harmony to the point of ascension. No longer does the incarnational personality wait to leave the earth-plane to achieve a finer or more harmonious existence, for 'heaven is here on earth'. The Law of Ascension means that we are meant to bring our loving energies to our everyday existence and to serve as models for others to emulate. We will recognize this ascendant energy in others by noting the degree to which other ascendant and non-ascendant beings are attracted to them.

6. The Law of Attraction

The Law of Attraction unites love and soul providing the universal harmony that is the foundation for all manifestation.

One of the Three Major Laws, the Law of Attraction is broken down into eleven subsidiary laws that compel the force of attraction holding our universe as well as our lives together. It is the Law of Attraction that holds our solar system to the Sirian and keeps our planets revolving around our central unit, the sun.

The Law of Attraction is the energy that spins the earth and holds molecular, atomic, and subatomic matter ever circulating around their centres. It is the primary law of man achieved through the synthesis of Love and Soul elements.

7. The Law of Balance

Also known as the Law of Fair Exchange, the Law of Balance or Equipoise is the law that supersedes all man's laws and creates stability for all third dimension manifestation. We get what we give; this is the principle of fair exchange.

Divine wisdom tells us that each thought must be balanced by the thinker. We must allow all viewpoints without letting the views of others dominate us, for each of us must make his own journey. Do not give away power easily, but give love unconditionally. Low self-esteem is just as non-productive as high self-esteem. They both deny equality. There is no salvation in extremes as we see in the manifestation of imbalance in addictive and compulsive personalities. Any message communicated with love validates equality and achieves balance.

8. The Law of Challenge

Just as there is a difference between being aggressive and being assertive, there is a difference between insulting and challenging a disembodied being.

When we encounter a disembodied being we have the right to ask his or her intent, identity, and whatever else we truly feel is pertinent. Those whose role it is to provide information to channelers do not mind being challenged, and if asked three times, in the same exact words each time, they will give accurate information.

9. The Law of Cohesion

Divine coherence is demonstrated in the molecular plane and manifested throughout the universe as the Law of Cohesion, one of the seven laws of the solar system. The Law of Cohesion is the source of universal unity and the home of the Monad.

10. The Law of Colour

Humans (hue-light; man-being) are composed of light, which in its purest sense, consists of colour, tone, symbol and vibration. All colours are centres of attraction whether they are complimentary or conflicting, and all colour impacts the physical, emotional, mental and human body profoundly. When rays of one or more colours are directed to a specific area of the body, change occurs.

11. The Law of Common Ground

Problems cannot be resolved by force or by compromise as one side invariably loses and will, as the saying goes, "come back to fight another day". The Law of Common Ground dictates that problems can be truly resolved when two or more ascendant beings gather together in a site that has been cleansed to blend their differences to reach a common goal.

Cleanse the area to be utilized of any residual energy from those who may have resided in or passed through it by caging it with a gold net and sending loving energy to the area for a period of time. This period will vary depending on who, historically speaking, has inhabited the space, the energy left behind, and the nature of the conflict you honestly wish to resolve. If the issue you wish to address is surrounded by contentious energy or residual negative energy inhabits the space, some time may be required.

12. The Law of Consciousness

As consciousness expands, so does our perspective; the space for events to transpire (possibility) increases and therefore the dimensions in which man recognizes good and evil, opportunity and possibility, past-present and future all expand to reveal the limits of prior perception and the real needs of this present world cycle.

13. The Law of Continuity of Consciousness

Cosmic consciousness creates an ever-expanding reality, and everything in creation is connected to everything else. The Universe is in a continuous and endless process of creation as the fusion of individual consciousness and the universal consciousness (the building of the antahkarana) results in the development of universal knowledge known as omniscience (all science/all knowledge). The medium for the 'implicit order' of this relationship is continuity. Achieving enlightenment requires that we be vigilant, observant of our context and surroundings in order to gain awareness of the larger context and to align ourselves within the cosmic continuity.

14. The Law of Cycles

As a part of nature we live within the pattern of larger cycles. We see them in the passing of seasons, in the continual passing of day to night, and in the waxing and waning of the moon. We cannot push the river; neither can we call back the tide. Universal timing is perfect, and all things that should happen, happen in 'good' time. It does not pay to despair or rejoice beyond measure for whatever rises falls, whatever fulls, empties. Nothing is forever; this is the principle of cycles.

15. The Law of Divine Invocation

"Under the Law of Grace" keeps us from unintentionally manifesting or invoking anything that would harm us, our karma and/or others. This law is not for the self-serving, for those want for self rather than for service will find the law overruled by self-interest.

For those who sincerely desire to do no harm and particularly for those working in the service of others, the Law of Divine Invocation allows the ascended realms to move from the confines of the Law of Non-Intervention to act on our behalf.

Invoke the Divine Decree three times by saying:

"By Divine Decree," in the name of _____ I ask for_____.

It is done and I thank you.

Or "Under the Law of Grace," in the name of _____ I ask for_____.

It is done and I thank you.

Repeat one (not both) of the request three times, and then let it go. Trust that it is in higher hands.

16. The Law of Discipline

Discipline is the surest means to the greatest freedom and independence.

Discipline enables us to focus and achieve the knowledge and skills that translate into more and better options in life. It is the muscle of the enlightened body, not because discipline is overbearing or rigid, but because it provides the strength of character and commitment that are the foundations of enlightened living. Discipline without commitment is a stab in the dark, not the bridge between here and where we want to be.

17. The Law of Divine Flow

"Ease up!" "Go with the flow!" "Get in synch!"—good advice for those stressed out and out of step with conscious living.

Living in the moment and centring ourselves in love and service to others (as opposed to service of self), we live within the Law of Divine Flow. When we stay in the moment by moment flowing of our higher selves, creating actions which reflect love and possibility, we notice how we say just the right things, do what is best for all, and refrain from doing that which we previously disliked in ourselves or others. We maintain a stronger connection to our God-self as we focus on the here-and-now rather than worrying about of trying to unduly manipulate the future. The more we do this, the more we are able to do this. To a degree, deliberately going against the flow means we have allowed our spiritual integrity to be compromised.

18. The Law of Divine Love and Oneness

When we, as ascendant beings, complete a round of reincarnation, we develop such soul growth that the vibrational speed of our being qualifies us to merge with God. We then become a soul extension of God, and among the many choices we have we may opt to live in the liquid light which flows in and from God, or reincarnate as an avatar in third dimensional existence with the purpose of aiding mankind.

19. The Law of Economy

The Law of Economy causes matter to always follow the line of least resistance, and this is the basis of the "separative" action of atomic matter atoms scatter from each other and in so doing create a vibratory rhythm attuned to the heterogeneity and quality inherent in rotary action. The Law of Economy governs matter and is the opposite pole of spirit. Initiates must master this law before they can achieve liberation and enlightenment.

20. The Law of Economy of Force

The initiate who aims to provide a point of contact between conditions of chaos and the initiate who works for constructive ends and order must ascribe to the Economy of Force in all they do. This requires due discrimination and a true sense of values. The result is the economizing of time and effort; energy is distributed wisely, excess is eliminated, and thus the aspirant can be relied upon by the Great Ones as a true and able helper.

One of the Three Major Laws, the Law of Economy of Force influences Activity. This is the law that adjusts the equilibrium between the material and spiritual evolution of the cosmos, ensuring that energy is expended to its best possible end with the minimum of force. Unevenness of rhythm is an illusion of time and does not exist in the cosmic centre which is perfectly balanced and aligned.

In knowing this, we find peace in all its connotations, peace that contains the next racial expansion of consciousness hidden within its meaning.

21. The Law of Equalities (or Analogy)

Experiential reality- life as we know it or think we know it, is but a reflection of the condition of the soul: our outer experience is basically equal to our innermost perception of ourselves and our place in the grand scheme of things. As within, so without. The thoughts and images we hold in our conscious and subconscious minds manifest their mirror likenesses in our external circumstances.

The Laws and Phenomena of the various planes of Being correspond to various aspects of life, and the Law of Equalities, also known as Principle of Correspondence or Essential Divinity enable the phenomena of Discernment, Intuition, Hunches, etc. and that which is called remote viewing or out of body experience. Earth is a school for practicing these laws of mind control while maintaining a connection to all being.

Correspondence establishes the interconnectedness between all things in the universe and keeps all things relative to each other. Known to the adepts and masters of ancient Egypt as the substance of the ethereal and the spirit substance or web that pervades and interpenetrates the universe, the substance of the ethereal acts as a medium for the transmission of light, heat, electricity and gravity. Non-material in nature, it is also known as the un-created substance, or universal substance.

First discovered on Earth while scientists were conducting research with the Hubble space telescope spirit-substance is manifesting in the ethers. It is the beginning of matter. This is the lifeforce in which all suns, worlds, and galaxies are suspended in space, time and change. Science refers to this substance as "dark matter" that cannot be seen, touched, smelled, or weighed. Dark matter does not absorb or reflect light and is therefore invisible. It is considered a non-material substance present in each of the three Planes of Correspondence, also known as the ascending scale of life and being and the Trinity of Being: The Great Spiritual Plane; The Great Mental Plane; The Great Physical Plane.

We are all intimately connected via this dark matter of essential being, whether we realize it or not. Dark matter is the source of love-wisdom and the major linking agent in the universe that leads us back toward the sense of oneness and enlightenment.

22. The Law of Expansion

It is a fact in nature that all existence dwells within a sphere. This is the law of a gradual evolutionary expansion. The consciousness dwelling in every life form is the cause of the spheroid-like form of all life in the solar system. The law of relativity, or the relation between all atoms, produces that which is called Light which in its aggregated phenomena, forms a composite sphere, known a solar system. The sphere requires two types of force - rotary and spiral-cyclic to produce its own internal activity.

The Law of Expansion is also known as the Law of Expansive Response, and its symbol is the flaming rosy sun with a sign symbolizing the union of fire and water in the centre. The ray energy is the expansive energy of the 3rd ray, the adapting factor.

23. The Law of Expectation

We can move toward what we can see, but we cannot exceed the bounds of our own imaginations. Energy follows thought thus allowing our deepest thoughts, for better or for worse, to manifest. Our fundamental assumptions, expectations and beliefs, however, colour and create our experience. Only by changing our fundamental expectations can we change our outcomes.

24. The Law of Faith

We know more than we know, we have hunches, intuitions, and visions of a whole that is larger than the sum of what we have read, heard or studied. Déjà vu is nothing more than the recollection of the larger collective unconscious: the universal ALL that we are all a part of.

Each of us, explains renowned psychologist, Carl Gustav Jung, holds a pool of collective, universal knowledge within our subconscious; this is universal knowledge. We have only to look within, listen, discern, and trust our inner, universal knowledge. We must learn to differentiate between our outward desires and biases to objectively access our deepest intuitions and to rely on intuitive knowledge as the ultimate arbitrator in all of our decisions. Faith in the collective body of universal knowledge is the key to the Law of Faith.

25. The Law of Flexibility

Acceptance of our selves and others for what they are without drama or bias means embracing and making constructive use of the moment—even if it wasn't our finest. It is the only moment that IS. Our actions and reactions define us.

Everything serves the highest good if we make the best possible use of it. This requires an alert and expansive state of awareness as well as the ability to lay ego to one side. Stumbling blocks become stepping stones and problems become opportunities. This is the basic foundation of personal growth and true spiritual development. We must have, as the Buddha advised and 12 step programs around the world remind us, "the serenity to accept the things we cannot change, the courage to change the things we can, and the wisdom to know the difference."

26. The Law of Forgiveness

When we see all as love we build the energy of allowingness we realize that in the full process of time, all things are forgiven. Thus we lose the need for retribution or revenge. By forgiving we release old anger and open the way for the Law of Grace to intercede and dispense away with negative karma we may have accumulated in the Akasha. The old energy of 'an eye-for-an-eye" on the other hand keeps our personal vibrations at their lowest and keeps us trapped in the past.

Forgiveness is an eternal virtue that holds the universe together.

All good comes from forgiveness. The human species continues life here and hereafter because of God's ultimate forgiveness and thus forgiveness, though not easy, is duly recompensed as a holy act. Forgiveness, not punishment, is the might of those who are truly mighty, and forgiveness and gentleness are the qualities of the self-possessed.

27. The Law of Free Will

The goal of the ascendant being is to voluntarily and willingly surrender the ego, hanging up the Soul-Overcoat of manifestation in order to become a perfected spirit regardless of how many lifetimes it takes. However, each of us in this regard has free will and free choice. We have the power to choose our direction—towards or away from the universal light and harmony—no matter what our circumstances, just as we choose to be under the power of others or an example to others.

The mind builds the thoughts that influence our choices manifest in the hundreds of actions and reactions that lead us to the circumstances we find ourselves in today. Our choices influence our experience, and our experience again influences our minds. It is a cycle, but whether a vicious cycle or not depends largely on the choices we make. Just as Adam and Eve had the choice to eat of the forbidden fruit, and even as their choice affected human experience irrevocably and forever, we face choices daily that only seem to be of less consequence. They are, in fact, tantamount. These "small choices" determine whether we live in the darkness or the light.

We in third dimension have the right to expand or contract, to bring our creative and expressive energies out into the world in positive or negative ways. This is our ultimate decision. The free will we use to create our choices mixes with our ability to love profoundly, and therefore the law of free will determines the amount of time we will spend in the attempt to merge with the Great Soul of all Creation.

28. The Law of Gender

All life forms contain the two elements of gender—masculine and feminine—yin and yang. On the great physical plane, the sexes of all species are manifested as male and female. On the great mental plane, gender manifests as masculine and feminine energies that exist within each and every person. Every male has its female element, and every female has its male element. On the great spiritual plane, gender manifests as the Father-Mother principle of the Infinite Omnipresent God in whose mind the universe is conceived and firmly held. It is written, "We all live, move, and have our being within God." When balance and learning reach a critical mass, the personality achieves the merger with God, and we see self as neither male nor female, but as one blended self.

This law embodies the Truth that gender is manifested in everything; masculine and feminine are ever at work on all planes of causation, just surely as protons (+) and electrons (-) are constantly at work in the atom. Gender manifests on all three planes of causation which are the great spiritual plane, the great mental plane, and the great physical plane. The law is always the same on all planes, but on the higher planes, it takes higher forms of manifestation. This law works in the direction of generation, regeneration, and creation.

29. The Law of Good Will

The will-to-good of the world knowers is the magnetic seed of the future." Our mental capacity today readily connects to those universal ideas which constitute the purpose behind the form. We each have the ability to mentally construct a happening, and see it through to completion. This is the "will-to-good." The will-to-good is always an education process where the recipients are left free to receive the idea or not. The responsibility for expanding the amount of goodwill in the world rests directly on the shoulders of the intelligentsia of the world. In the goodwill process it is the creative/idea/problem solving individuals who are directly responsible for creating goodwill.

In an energy relationship there is always a positive, creating side and a negative, receiving side of that creative relation. This is simply how the world works. The will-to-good is the positive, creative impetus, which, when received, makes the manifestation of goodwill possible. We are either mentally polarized or emotionally polarized. However, only those who are mentally polarized can begin to appropriate this energy through will on the mental plane. When this is fully comprehended, we begin to realize why the manifestation of goodwill is not more widespread.

30. The Law of Grace

No sincere effort goes unnoticed, and the Law of Grace allows those who truly seek the greater good special dispensation: the Law of Karma may be waived to the diligent and loving earthhealer who works in good faith but forgets to put change in her parking meter. The Law of Grace intervenes, when needed and appropriate, to allow us a dispensation from any negative consequences of a karma incurrence and it ensures we do not interfere with another's soul plan.

To benefit from the law of grace requires that we live in grace and that our efforts are sincere. It cannot be abused or it disappears leaving the would-be user with the repercussions—a fall from grace as it were.

Those who by virtue of their endeavours and service to others merit occasional graceful intervention can invoke the law simply by inserting in the request, "Under the Law of Grace…"

31. The Law of Group Endeavour

There is power in numbers. Whenever like-minded individuals come together to pray, manifest, do light-work, or even to create degrees of control we define as evil or black magic, their power is multiplied. Where the efforts of an individual may equal one unit, the efforts of two praying or healing for a common goal with equal energy will affect the energy of twenty units instead of the sum total of two. With three, the resultant energy explodes further.

The Law of Group Endeavour defines the multiplying of energy created when like minds and like hearts work in unison.

32. The Law of Group Life

No being exists in isolation; the choices we manifest in our thoughts are but one thread in the infinite tapestry of life, a small part of a whole that includes the rest of humanity. We must, then, look beyond ourselves, our families, and even our communities and nations to think in terms of the greater good of the universe itself. Fairness and fair play are universal, and the initiate cannot seek benefit to self that results in a detriment to the "group" or any of the individuals that make it up. This is the Law of Brotherhood or the Law of Group Life. We must consider our actions and our thoughts in light of universal questions: Is it the truth (for everyone, not just one group or individual)? Is it fair to all involved? Will it be of benefit to all?

Practice makes perfect, and with practice, thinking and acting within the group context and in the groups best interests will gradually become part of our collective consciousness. As civilization adjusts itself to these new conditions self-aggrandizement ceases to be the sole focus of governments and individuals. All aspects of life are interdependent, and when one proceeds to fuller, more universal thinking all of the group, including the original thinker benefit in manifold.

33. The Law of Healing

"We are but the hands of God, here to do His work." Hands-on healers, whose brain waves reverberate the Earth's pulse (7.8 Hz) channel energy to remove blockages or instil the sacred energy to the past, present or future. The Law of Healing also enables us to heal ourselves in the third dimension by virtue of a leap of faith: the faith that we are already healed.

34. The Law of Higher Will

When we surrender our smaller self and will to the guidance of a higher will and dedicate our actions for the highest good of ALL concerned, we feel an inspired glow at the centre of our lives. It is this feeling that enables us to move beyond our separate selves and smaller wills to relinquish control to the Higher Will whose knowledge and wisdom is infinitely greater than our own.

35. The Law of Honesty

Whether we like it or not, we tend to be self-cantered and we tend to act in our own best interests. If we have to lie to ourselves to do so we are likely to be surprised how gullible we are when it comes to accepting a 'convenient lie'.

Only when we are completely honest with ourselves about ourselves can we speak or act honestly with others. Furthermore, integrity and honesty require that we go beyond thought to act in line with higher laws despite strong impulses to the contrary. These impulses are but the yipping of latent self-interest.

Fear is no excuse. When we let fear stop us from expressing our true feelings and needs, we are being dishonest with ourselves and it costs us a sense of energy and spirit.

There is no punishment for acting in contravention of spiritual and higher laws such as the Law of Honesty. Breaking the law is its own punishment as it changes vibrational levels of our spirit energy and sets into motion subtle forces whose natural consequences we cannot escape any more than we can escape the force of gravity.

36. The Law of Identity

Inherent in the Law of Identity is the unique right each of us has to create our own identity. This is often called "being-ness". Our identity spans "lifetimes" and includes time between incarnations as well as third-dimensional incarnational experiences. Furthermore, identity does not cease when an entity merges with the Great Centre, as we may again separate to accomplish a goal in our former individual identity.

37. The Law of Intention

"Words without deeds are dead," we are told, and the same holds true for thoughts. Energy must follow intention or that which is perceived will not take place. All that holds us back from action in a worthy cause—fear, sloth, selfishness and so forth—constitutes bad intent.

The Law of Intention also speaks to motives. When we speak to "sound good" but fail to follow through, just as when we act but act for purposes of recognition or self-benefit our motives and our energy are skewed. No good can come of poor intentions. Intention and effort must be sincere (of higher vibration) to achieve genuine spiritual growth or reward.

38. The Law of Intuition

We can only know and act on our own intuition and inner wisdom when we trust our inner selves and feelings over the dictates and authority of others. We must trust and value our own intuition and have a sense of our own identity in order to hear our inner voices over the clamour of the crowd. When we know ourselves, we hear ourselves. Our intuition becomes more profound when have claimed our own sacred identity.

39. The Law of Justice

Justice rings to the farthest reaches of the known universe and beyond. Those who are just have banished forever all thwarting crosscurrents of ego. Those who are unjust will find no place to hide. The Law of Justice is instantaneous and when violated the universe conspires for retribution. This we know as karma.

40. The Law of Karma

Every cause has its' effect; every effect has its cause. Chance is but a name for law not recognized. There are many planes of causation, but nothing escapes the law. It is ever at work with chains of causations and effects that govern all of life and manifested matter.

The karmic law requires that every human wish find ultimate fulfilment. Therefore, desire is the chain that binds man to the reincarnation wheel. Karma is attracted only where the magnet of the personal ego still exists. An understanding of karma as the law of justice underlying life's inequalities serves to free the human mind from resentment against God and man.

The law itself is illusive and cannot be proven other than observed with the mind and is used to determine the causations and effects of specific events. When this law is used with conscious effort, desired results can be produced in a person's life. These effects steer us along definite paths of causation. When the law is used by an unconscious and haphazard mind, the effects are potentially disastrous for the individual or group of individuals. So called "accidents" could occur without warning to individuals who toil through life without awareness.

Because there are seven dimensions of reality in which causations can occur, we remain unaware of many reasons for effects. By understanding Universal laws we can learn to operate in grace instead of accumulating karma. This law is mechanically or mathematically operative; its workings may be scientifically manipulated by men and women of divine wisdom who are fully realized.

Karma can be understood to the observing mind which sees the cycles in all things, and realizes that all things follow the Great Law. We are responsible for the very thoughts that we produce are the final result of our own mental alchemy. In every minute thought, action, and deed that is performed, we set into motion unseen chains of causation and effect which will vibrate from the mental plane throughout the entire cellular structure of body, out into the environment, and finally into the cosmos. Eventually the vibratory energy returns to its originator upon the return swing of the pendulum. And all this takes less time than the twinkling of an eye.

41. The Law of Knowledge

Knowledge is energy that can be applied, used or misused. As the consequences of misuse can be dire, much information is withheld from initiates. It is not until the initiate achieves the knowledge and status of the pledged disciple that more will be revealed.

In-depth knowledge is not required for the initiate to progress to higher levels. All that is required is: 1) the right apprehension of energy: its sources, qualities, types and vibrations and 2) the right apprehension of the laws of energy and conservation of force. The Law of Knowledge dictates that due knowledge shall arrive to the seeker in due time.

42. The Law of Love

To understand love we must differentiate between love that is desire—love in the personality, love that is magnetic and love that is transformative. Each phase marks a period of completion; each is a starting point for fresh endeavours in life. Thus the soul migrates from the personality and back again to its source. From this perspective we see that there is a vast difference between love and desire which limits love.

43. The Law of Magnetic Control

Every thought we have creates a match that comes back to us like a boomerang, and in the development of the control of this law lies hidden the control of the personality by the Monad via the egoic body.

One of the seven laws of our solar system, under the three major laws, The Law of Magnetic Control dictates that our thoughts, especially thoughts on the Buddhic plane are charged with energy. Furthermore, like energies attract. Thus our thoughts are galvanized to their correlatives; every thought has the potential to grow. We see this in the principal of "the eleventh monkey" that posits that like thoughts combine until it requires only one more thought to galvanize them into a reality on the material plane.

44. The Law of Magnetic Impulse

Also known as the Law or Polar Union whose symbol is two fiery balls united by a triangle of fire, the Law of Magnetic Impulse is the manifesting factor and the first step towards universal union.

The Law of Magnetic Impulse results in an eventual union between the man and the group which produces harmonious group relations.

45. The Law of Magnetism

The Law of Magnetism speaks to the unifying of the personality. It is an expression of lunar force. The Law of Magnetism has three distinct phases: the stage of intellectuality or artistic attainment, the stage of discipleship, and the stage known as Treading the Path. By completing each of these stages we affect a synthesis and unify the energies commonly associated with attraction.

46. The Law of Manifestation

Although invisible, thought is a force just as electricity and gravitation are forces. The human mind is a spark of the almighty consciousness of God. Whatever the powerful mind (holding a pure thought - that which excludes any other thought) believes very intensely will instantly come to pass. There are actions, sounds, techniques, mental energy and symbols which when understood enable us to manifest energy (love, joy, peace, etc.) into our auras. With practice and increased love held in the heart and emotional body we are eventually able to manifest physical objects.

47. The Law of Mantras

Through the mantra we connect and become one with the Higher Being. Each mantra is linked to a certain manifestation of the absolute Divinity, and in true mantra practice, when we forget the self-chanting to become the mantra itself; we attain a state where nothing but the mantra exists.

Thus we connect. The mantra represents the name of a Master Being and connects us to the ray of light emanating from that being. We connect through the sounds "aum," 'om," "hu," etc. with a resonance and frequency that is profoundly beneficial in raising the vibration of the self.

48. The Law of Meditation

This is the law of current or unified thought that is a continuum of mental effort aimed at assimilating the object of meditation. It is free from any other thought. Time does not exist and what we refer to as past and future have no bearing on the mental plane. Time becomes a convention of thought and language a social agreement. Truth lies in the moment—this moment—the only moment that actually exists. Anxiety about past and future only serve to maintain the anxiety, as the mental pictures we create then manifest in our lives. When we practice remembering that the here and now is all we have, our present moments improve.

49. The Law of Process

Enlightenment is a process, not an event. Whether we reach nirvana within this reincarnation cycle or not, meditating calms the inner self. At its most profound the Law of Process culminates in the merging with the God-source or "enlightenment" as the Buddhists would call it.

50. The Law of Mentalism

The mind is ALL. ALL is the mind. It is spirit indefinable, unknowable, and thought of as a universal, infinite, living mind. The ALL consists of all universal knowledge, the substantial reality underlying all the outward empirical manifestations. The material universe, phenomena, matter, energy and all that is apparent to our material senses is part of the ALL.

The Law of Mentalism explains the true nature of energy, power and matter. The Universe is mental in nature. The atom of matter, the unit of force, the mind of man, and the being of the arch-angel are all but degrees in one scale, and all fundamentally the same. The difference is solely a matter of degree and rate of vibration. All are creations of the All, and have their existence solely within the Infinite Mind of the All. Mental transmutation is the art of changing the conditions of the universe, along the lines of matter, force, and mind.

51. The Law of Miracles

All events in our precisely adjusted universe are lawfully wrought and lawfully explicable. The socalled miraculous powers of a great master are but the natural accompaniments to his or her exact understanding of subtle laws that operate in the inner cosmos of the consciousness. Nothing is a miracle, yet in the truest sense, everything is a miracle. Is anything more miraculous than that each of us is encased in an intricately organized body, and is set upon on earth whirling through space among the stars?

The Law of Miracles is operable by any person who has realized that the essence of creation is light. A master is able to employ his/her divine knowledge of light phenomena to project instantly into perceptible manifestation the ubiquitous light atoms. The actual form of the projection (whatever it is water into wine, medicine, a human body) is determined by the master's wish and limited only by his or her powers of will and visualization.

52. The Law of No Judgments

We are not judged, nor should we judge. The Universal Spirit does not judge, for judgments are human inventions: a means to compare, contrast, and above all, control as we measure ourselves and others against shallow and idealistic standards of perfection, morality and truth. Judgment attracts judgment, and under the Law of Equities: so as we judge, so shall we be judged. The only real assessment is that we conduct upon ourselves after death as a condition of living in the duality of the third dimension.

53. The Law of Non-Attachment

Enlightenment is non-attachment. The ultimate nature of the self is Empty. The self does not exist as a separate entity. Attachment to the self creates karma. Non-attachment to the self dissolves karma.

A full conceptual understanding needs to occur, as mere conceptual understanding that the self is empty and, hence, detached does not lead to liberation. Many methods have been devised to help human beings attain this realization. These usually fall into two categories. The first is 'nonattached behaviour' and the other is called 'spiritual practice.' Through diligent application of these methods, an individual can free him or herself from the confines of judgment to achieve that which is real and attainable, his true karma-determined existence.

54. The Law of Non-Intervention

The karma repercussions of intervention are dire, indeed. The Law of Non-intervention dictates that no spirit is allowed to channel material to a recipient that would force a change in the evolution of that person. Although we can accept intervention from another source by going into a trance and allowing our consciousness to leave for another to enter and impart knowledge, we cannot force our knowledge or interventions on others.

The Law of Non-intervention concerns the individual and group right to serve self rather than to live in the vibration of service to others. This law prevents physical and non-physical beings from intervening to correct what they see as wrong or harmful in others, as doing so would rob them of the chance to auto-correct and address their karma in the process.

55. The Law of One

The universe is ONE. The Lord is ONE. All that is, was, and will be has its being in the ONE. So it is with life. So it is with consciousness. The enlightened being lives within the ONENESS of that Universal Consciousness on Earth.

56. The Law of Order of Creation

Creation is yin and yang, darkness and light. All that exists is conceived in spirit and grows in the light of the mental plane before it is manifested in the material. All begins as light. However, the children of God and the Children of Men direct and force the light into channels for power, turning it into a destructive, dark force. Whereas man has leaned towards the dark for many centuries, the balance of light and dark is shifting. We are now reaching the turning point where the light shall exceed the darkness.

57. The Law of Patience

Every soul is unique and each will come to its enlightenment in its own time. We cannot force that onto the being which is not YET meant to be. Through Patience we know ourselves; we test our ideals and realize that the faults we find in others are faults we know from prior experience. Patiently we seek true understanding. As Luke says, "In your patience possess ye your souls."

Patience requires spiritual, mental, and physical thought and action, and through patience we learn faith and understanding. Patience allows all other virtues to manifest more profoundly, proportional to the patience we exercise in the process.

58. The Law of Patterns

Our ability to make change is largely dictated by the ways we learn when we are young. We learn to make sense of the world by observing patterns, and this has survival value. However, patterns quickly transform into habits, both good and bad.

We can reward good habits in due proportion while retaining our spontaneity: we can be open to positive change, to doing old things in new ways and to restructuring our lives and our behaviours to achieve positive growth. We can and should examine our patterns and correct those we find dysfunctional, negative, or destructive. "Every action has an equal and opposite reaction," and any habit or pattern, whether we call it good or bad, tends to reassert itself over time unless we break that pattern by doing something different—something that will have enough impact to interrupt the old pattern.

59. The Law of Perfection

From a transcendental perspective, everyone and everything is unconditionally perfect. From a conventional viewpoint, perfection does not exist. Excellence is the best we can achieve, and achieving it takes time and practice. However, although perfection itself may be difficult to obtain, The Law of Perfection speaks to the perfectness of our unfolding. Despite wrong turns and ups and downs, our journey towards perfection is perfect in itself if we are in tune with the universal spirit and our karma. As long as we are "unfolding" we are progressing "perfectly." When we understand the larger picture, we understand our role and responsibility in helping the world we live in to become more loving, giving, kinder and gentler, we live up to this responsibility and expand into the perfection of our higher selves.

60. The Law of Periodicity

Rhythm, ebb and flow, are the measured beat of the pulsating life and the law of the universe. In learning to respond to the vibration of the high Places, this rhythmic periodicity must be borne in mind. Training for the aspirant will by cyclic, and will have its ebb and flow, as all else in nature. Times of activity are followed by times of pralaya, and periods of registered contact alternate with periods of apparent silence. If the student develops as desired, each pralayic period is succeeded by one of greater activity, and of more potent achievement.

61. The Law of Polarity

Everything is dual. Everything is polarized. Like and unlike are but two sides of the same coin.Opposites are different in degree but identical in nature. All paradoxes can be reconciled within the whole. Without the law of polarity - light, gravity and electricity would not be possible.

The law of cause and effect is closely connected to polarity and holds us true to the choices we make and the actions we take by returning to us what we have measured out to others. Like the swing of the pendulum, our energy always returns where it began. In biblical terms it is expressed as, "Whatsoever a man sows, so shall he reap" and "Do unto others, as you would have them to you."

The evidence of this principle is observed in the polarity of planets and the various celestial bodies that include our earth, solar system, and galaxy. On the mental plane, this principle manifests itself in the heart-centre of each person as the enlightened mind. The Principle of Polarity makes possible the choices we make on the scale of life between good and evil, right and wrong, generosity and greed, love and fear, truth and lies.

The law of cause and effect is closely connected to polarity and holds us true to the choices and actions we make by returning to us what we have measured out to others. Like the swing of the pendulum, it always returns where it began.

62. The Law of the Present Moment

We must all be aware that we have goals—things seemingly great and small to accomplish within our lives. Whether our goals are small or large is of little consequence. Even the most daunting achievement can be managed in increments or "baby steps."

At the same time, the Law of the Present Moment tells us that there are no shortcuts. If we skip a single step the results are likely to be a failure. Skipping steps is a sure sign of impatience with the process. Instead, we must learn to appreciate and live in the moment. Big or small, the step we are taking NOW is the only step in the present moment, hence the only step that matters.

63. The Law of Progress

The universe is in a state of constant growth, and progress can be made in all directions; flux is at the heart of progress. We can progress in the pathways of good or evil. The informing consciousness is also in a constant state of change, and this informing consciousness is seen in the deva kingdom and in certain pranic energies. The Law of Progress dictates that what is needful will come into being.

64. The Law of Prophecy

The future is happening, unfolding in the "I AM." We are perpetually in the state of "NOW." The only true future that exists is the desire or will of the Source of all Creation that none shall be lost.

Sacred geometry is a manifestation of God's love. People who are able to tune into the Akashic records and the Universal Consciousness sometimes map a line from the supposed past to the present and then to the future. The ability to use sacred geometry comes with the raising of vibration to such a degree that the personality gains the right to assess Akasha for the good of another or of self.

When reading the energy going to the future of people on earth we must keep in mind, however, that energy changes from moment to moment. While those powerful prophets of old were correct in their time and some of what they said has held true to present day, many of their prophecies have lost relevancy. The Law of Prophecy suggests we be sceptical of prophecy due to the complex and ever changing nature of the universe. Furthermore, just by hearing prediction, we change the outcome to some degree, thus rendering our 'prophecy' automatically irrelevant.

65. The Law of Radiation

Liberation means the ability of any conscious atom to pass out of one sphere of energized influence into another of a higher vibration and thus manifesting a larger and wider expanse of conscious realization.

Understanding the radiatory or emancipatory condition of all substances as a specific point in evolution allows us to approach Reality. The Law of Radiation governs the outer effect produced by all forms in all kingdoms. When their internal activity has reached such a stage of vibratory activity that the confining walls of the form no longer form a prison, the Law of Radiation permits the liberation of the subjective essence. Liberation means the ability of any conscious atom to pass out of one sphere of energized influence into another sphere of a higher vibration and a larger and wider expanse of conscious realization.

66. The Law of Rebirth

This law, when understood, will do much to solve the problems of sex and marriage for those who understand the true nature of life-as-continuum tread more carefully down its paths. Those who understand the Law of Rebirth know that each life represents a mass of ancient obligations requiring the recovery of old relations. Each evolving soul seeks the opportunity to pay old debts, a chance to make restitution and progress. This often requires the awakening of deep-seated qualities, the recognition of old friends and enemies, the solution of revolting injustices and the understanding of that which conditions the man and makes him what he is.

67. The Law of Rebound

The Law of Rebound enables us to come out of negative situations stronger, wiser, and bolder. If we do not gain a clear victory or even if we are utterly defeated, the soul grows in the process. We have seen this in stories since the beginning of mankind. The initiate who understands the Law of Rebound may lose the battle, but still win the war. By trying we build wisdom and resilience that will stand us in good stead, even if we fail. Traumatic situations often create the need for rebound, and the soul sees in these negative occurrences of the opportunity to give self and others to affect a leap in faith.

68. The Law of Responsibility

Acting responsibly requires that we establish the limits and boundaries of our responsibility, taking full charge of that which is our duty and letting go of that which is not. We find more enjoyment supporting others as we create more harmonious co-operative relationships by understanding and focusing exclusively on that which falls within our realm of responsibility. Under this law we understand the need to over co-operate but NOT to the extent that we becomes co-dependent - the condition characterized by an obsessive focus on other people's lives. This law reminds us to respect our internal values and find our own point of balance.

69. The Law of Rhythm

The Law of Rhythm the most visible of all principles on the physical plane. Its power is reflected within the forces of nature which move the waves and tides of our oceans and cause the continuous changes of the seasons. The Law of Rhythm is observed in the continuous cycles of life and death, and in the rebirth of all things including the rise and fall of governments and nations and the constant creation and destruction of suns, worlds, and galaxies. Everything flows, out and in; everything has its "tides;" all things rise and fall; the pendulum-swing manifests in everything, and the measure of the swing to the right is the measure of the swing to the left; rhythm compensates.

Rhythm is the law of compensation and The Law of Rhythm maintains equilibrium in all things. It returns to us that which we give out in life. The return swing of the pendulum is assured without fail and there is no escape from the effects of this immutable law. The door of universal law swings in all directions. The final result depends what we have chosen to believe and whether or not our belief system allows us to see the truth as it really is. If we do not want to know the truth or do not care, we will evolve through the standard process of evolution. Nothing can, or is allowed to stand still.

All manifestation is the result of active energy producing certain results, and expenditure of energy in any one direction will necessitate an equal expenditure in an opposite direction.

This law holds us true to what we believe and compensates us accordingly. The pendulum-like swing of rhythm is immutable and we can only counteract its backward swing by mentally polarizing ourselves in a desirable position on the scale of life. It requires a dedicated personal commitment to cultivate the unknown within all of us in order to cause a quantum leap in the evolutionary process of life with all its aches and pains. This is a mental art that is known to hierophants, adepts, and masters of all ages. We will fulfil the Law of Rhythm one way or another, either by using the law to our advantage or by become its subject.

70. The Law of Right Human Relations

No man, or woman for that matter, is a prophet. No one has a franchise on reality; no one knows "the best way to do things." No one, then, can dictate to another. "Let no one assume to forcibly teach, counsel or guide, for we all have the greatest of these we could hope for already within us." The only being we can really counsel is the self. In our relationships we achieve greater results with others by our own fine example and by listening. People answer their own questions if given the opportunity. The only real control we ever have and need is the control of self.

And yet, there are those for whom teaching is a means to an end, be that control, self-avoidance or self-aggrandizement. These pseudo-teachers have no students—only victims. A strong action may be required to thwart such a teacher and become independent of another's will. The Law of Right Human Relations recognizes this right. We are all pupils and learners in the third dimension. By diverting our attentions to others and failing to search for excellence within, we lose sight of the gifts we already have, overlooking them in our haste to teach others.

71. The Law of Schools
(The Law of Love & Light)

As initiates who have transcended the stage of self-consciousness we are governed by the Law of Schools, also known as the Law of Love and Light. The consciousness does not expand helterskelter. As initiates we must undergo a transformation of consciousness including knowledge of the Higher Self required to produce alignment and illumination; the knowledge of our Guru or that which we seek to know; knowledge of the tools needed to conduct our work and service; and finally, knowledge of other souls with whom we can work. The Law of Schools is a mysterious term used to cover universal law as it affects the expansion of consciousness initiates undergo.

72. The Law of Service

The Law of Service grows naturally out of the successful application of the sciences of the antahkarana and meditation. It is the governing law of the future. Growth is achieved by forgetting self in the service of the race. With the linking of soul and personality the light of the soul pours into the brain consciousness, resulting in the subordination of the lower to the higher. This identification produces a corresponding activity in the personal life and an outpouring of the activity we call service. If the evasion of this law is a conscious action, there are karmic penalties. This work requires sacrifice of time and personal interest; it requires deliberate effort, conscious wisdom and the ability to work without attachment.

73. The Law of Solar Evolution

This law, the sum total of all the lesser Solar laws and activities is more properly subject matter for those who have moved beyond the initiate stage. They are too numerous to summarize here.

74. The Law of Sound

The release of energy in the atom is linked to the science of sound, meaning that every living thing in existence has a sound. Through knowledge of these sounds we can bring about change and evolve new forms of knowledge.

Healing with sound has proved effective as sound has the capacity to restore us to our harmonic patterns. Chanting, tuning forks, and music can all bring about great healing and change. This is enhanced geometrically by the Law of the Group. Chanting with a group heightens the effect of the mantra. The most powerful mantra presently known to man is the Dali Lama's favourite "Om mani padme hum," six syllables thought to be capable of purifying the six realms of existence.

75. The Law of Spiritual Approach

It is the goal of every conscious being to become a walking, talking example of the God-self. The Law of Spiritual Approach shows us that behind our every thought, word, action, and prayer is the Creator of All. When we learn to approach this spiritual being, we learn the correct spiritual approach for all situations and all beings: one of deference in respect. When we approach others and the Creator appropriately, our personalities become the reflection of the god-self for others to learn from and emulate. This is how we become our higher and better selves.

76. The Law of Spiritual Awakening

A basic level of self-control and stability is required to maintain the degree of effort required for the awakening of other states of awareness. Because such awakening brings with it higher forms of perception and power, self-centred misuse of the greater perception and power bears a proportionally graver karmic consequence. Spiritual Awakening brings with it the need for moral impeccability.

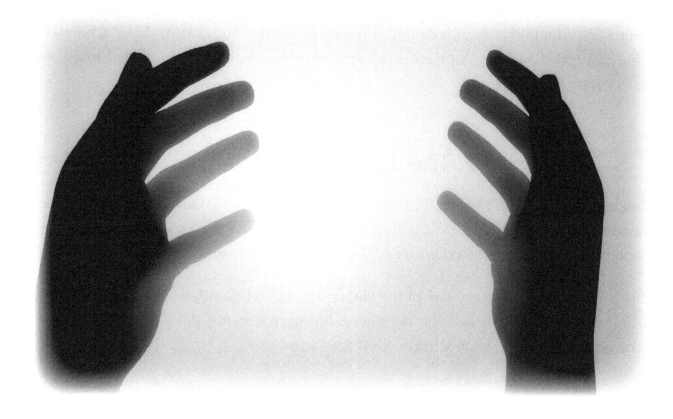

77. The Law of Summons

Through "soul-talk" and the Law of Summons we can learn how to relinquish the soul from the physical body and summon another soul with whom to have a soul-to-soul talk. The Law of Summons is one of the most powerful laws and requires that there be no conscious ego involved. Only thus can the message of love or the explanation of events from the perspective of a different soul be accepted profoundly in the manner it is intended.

78. The Law of Surrender

Until we have attained complete trust and faith in God we are likely to view surrender as a leap into the abyss or as death. Because we so cherish the self, relinquishing the ego is a very frightening experience. When we have absolute faith and trust, we accept that the self, once abandoned, merges with a higher stage of existence which is ready, willing and waiting for it. This is the "white light" of the next plane of existence near-death survivors see. It is the light of enlightenment and the white lotus flower that represents the unfolding of the universe as we merge with the God-light. At the time of surrender our entire being merges into the higher manifestation of reality in relation to what we have achieved in terms of our personal development. God streams into the soul that has created space with the negation of the self.

79. The Law of Synthesis

This is the concept of THE ONE. It is founded in the fact that all things, abstract and concrete stem from the God-source, are "units" of His thought, and are thus a concrete whole and not a differentiated process. Each "piece" of the whole is the whole.

This paradox is the primary law of the Heavenly Man who understands that each piece is the whole, the centre and the periphery. For such a being the Law of Economy is transcended and the Law of Attraction has full sway.

80. The Law of Teaching

Our future depends entirely on whether we learn to adapt to new more positive and holistic ways of thinking consistent with the positive energy in the universe—or not. Only then will we change from the old, dark ways of domination to new worlds of independence and interdependence. Without teaching and the assistance of the Great Masters past and present, it is unlikely that enough of a shift towards the light to effect dramatic and lasting change will be generated. The Law of Teaching encourages us, then, to share what we know and just as importantly to learn from others.

81. The Law of Telepathy

Through telepathy the fine vibrations of thoughts in one person's mind are transmitted through the subtle vibrations of astral ether and then through the grosser earthly ether, creating electrical waves which, in turn, translate themselves into thought waves in the mind of another person. The "third eye" or point between the eyebrows is the apparatus whereby thoughts are broadcast. However, they are heard in the heart. When the feeling of calm is concentrated in the heart, our psychic hearing is at its best. The heart acts as a mental radio, receiving the messages of others from far or near.

82. The Law of Three Requests

Whoso doubts the power of three simply isn't paying attention. Three is the Trinity, the number of magic wishes we get in fairy tales, the number of little pigs whose sagacity and building skills were tested by the big, bad wolf, and, as we all know, "the third time's the charm." Similarly, whenever we pray or request a higher power to assist us and whenever we invoke the Law of Grace, we bring stronger energy to the effort by repeating our request or prayer three times.

83. The Law of Time

The only moment we have is now. This is our realm; the "now" is where we are and where we create. What we have done is past, and when any cycle is completed that moment in history exists only as a record or energy trace in time and space. Third dimension linear time is for those living under the veil of forgetfulness. It allows them to centre on the moment and a perceived sense of order so they can avoid the burdens that come with the remembrance of past lives.

The consequences of past actions are atoned through karma, and can be rewritten to a degree, but only in the NOW. The FUTURE consists of today's thoughts, dressed by emotion and driven by action.

Activity is the key. Time is more rigid in the third than in the fourth dimension, yet only the most consciously evolved are able to master time. There are those who can slip into 'no time' but these are people who have raised their personal vibration by demonstrating many virtues, dispensing a great deal of positive karma and by relinquishing the ego entirely. They have spent years and lifetimes amassing the information and skill to suspend time.

84. The Law of Unconditional Love

Loving ourselves and other people as they are is a form of honouring the soul path of the self and the other. Loving without judgment or reservation creates the awareness that we are all part of God or the All. When we love without condition or restraint we connect profoundly with our higher selves. When we love unconditionally we notice that we say the right things at the right time; we're where we need to be when we need to be there, and life and events seem to flow to us in a more joyous and agreeable manner. Everything seems easier when living in unconditional love.

85. The Law of Unity

We all bear the seed of Divinity within us and are thus all connected to one another. This is the way we start, and the way we develop into eternity. It is only while in third dimension physical form where we are separated from our higher selves that we experience the illusion that we stand alone. Fear enters our emotional body because of this illusion and begins to close off our connection to the Source. When we experience great soul growth, in some small but profound manner, all souls throughout the universe benefit. All substance in this Universe flows to us and through us. We are All.

86. The Law of Vibration

Nothing rests; everything moves; everything vibrates. This is the law of progress, of movement and of rotation. One of the seven laws of our solar system, under the three major laws, the Law of Vibration is the law of progress, movement, and rotation. This Principal explains the differences in manifestations of matter, energy, mind and spirit, showing how each results from varying degrees and rates of vibration.

All that exists is in constant vibration and motion. Atoms vibrate so rapidly that they seem motionless to the physical eye. At the other end of the scale are things that vibrate so slowly that they also appear to be motionless or non-existent. In between are the various vibrations of living entities which range from consciousness all the way down to the lowly dust particle. And there are things even lower then dust. If we were to follow the scale of life all the way down to the utmost regions of the negative pole into pure undifferentiated matter, we again find ourselves in the realm of spirit - the Alpha and the Omega. All that is, begins in spirit and ends in spirit.

87. The Law of Will of God

God is all good, and it is by reason of the Good that all other things exist. It is God's will that what is human should be divine, and therefore all creation pushes forth to the God Light. God's working has to do with things free from change and movement - things divine. The creators of our world carry out their work of form-building under this law.

88. The Law of Will Power

This law depicts the right and condition of each personality or soul extension to generate its own degree of will power. As individuals developing soul extensions differ in degrees of will power from one to another, other entities, extensions and soul family members may not always agree with our will. Others in the soul family and/or other incarnational personalities (friends) may feel that our drive to accomplish something is overwhelming or obsessive. However, The Law of Will Power dictates that this is a question each of us must answer on our own. Answers will vary depending on the conditions of our incarnational experience and the objective of our will. If they are honest answers, gainfully sought through meditation chances are they are the right answers for our condition in the here-and-now. The Law of Will Power consistently shows us the right conditions under which we can and should exert our will.

PRACTICAL ASSIGNMENTS

Practical Assignment 1

It is no accident that I chose 88 universal laws to impart to you in this book. This number represents the masters from the Angelic Kingdom. In calling upon the loving support of the angelic kingdom, and in aligning with the Law of Miracles, what miracles are you powerfully requesting arrive at this moment in time in the most joyous, easy, miraculous way beyond what you ever could have hoped for or imagined.

List out the miracles that you are divinely commanding for your physical body, your mental and emotional body, your relationships (including yourself, your vocation and any other miracles that you would like to request at this time.)

Invoke the Law of Threes once you have completed your written request by writing, "thank you, amen, and so it is!"

Practical Assignment 2

I am a firm believer in the divine formula of aligned thought + aligned action = aligned results. If you applied this formula to the area of your life that does not seem to be manifesting as quickly as you would like, what is revealing itself in regards to the action that you need to take in order to consciously co-create the "and better"?

Set the intention that you are aligning with the Law of Action, call forward the wisdom of the 3 small, divinely aligned actions that you can take right now and write those down. Then, write out all of the things that will change (including how you feel) once these actions yields the results that you desire.

Practical Assignment 3

Create sacred time to list out the 3 Universal Laws that you feel most misaligned with. Write out what you are learning and how you are growing as a result of this 'misalignment'.

Then write out what you need to release (on an inner and outer level) in order to create greater alignment.

Lastly, write out who you need to become and what you need to call in to your life to create greater alignment with these laws.

Practical Assignment 4

Create sacred time to list out the Universal Laws that you feel most aligned with. Now, reflect on the wisdom that you have to share with others as a result of this alignment and write this down.

Then write out all of the people (groups or individuals) that can benefit most from this wisdom and create a plan of how you can reach them.

Practical Assignment 5

Create sacred space so that you can go inside and have a heart to heart with yourself about where you could benefit from taking action (i.e. your home, your career/business, your relationships, your health, etc.). Then tune in and write down below one small, next step action that you can take in each area to move your forward, when you will complete it, and how it will feel when you move forward on it.

Once complete, journal how it felt to complete the next steps, and then wash, rinse, repeat.

Practical Assignment 6

Take a moment to reflect on an inner conflict that you are having or a past or present conflict that you are experiencing with another person (i.e.. friend, parent, lover, etc). Go inside, set the intention that you are aligning with the Universal Law of Unconditional Love, and ask what will occur if you infuse that 'conflict' with the aligned wisdom of this law for the next 7 days.

Then, set aside a few moments each day to journal about what thoughts, memories, feelings and or shifts that you are noticing in regards to the conflict for the next days.

THANK YOU!

Thank you for taking this journey with me through some very powerful Universal Laws. If you would like to take your journey with me even further, be sure to visit http://www.souljourneys.ca/store/ to receive even more miracle-rich programs designed to support you on your soul's path.

Made in the USA
Columbia, SC
06 December 2021